The
WEDGE IN
THE DOOR

| YEAR 1942 | | AIRCRAFT | | PILOT, OR |
MONTH	DATE	Type	No.	1ST PILOT
Nov.	8	HUDSON	V-9095	SELF
Nov.	10	HUDSON	FH.448	SELF
Nov.	11	HUDSON	FH-357	SELF
Nov.	13	HUDSON	V.9129	SELF
Nov.	14	HUDSON	V.9129	SELF
Nov.	15	HUDSON	FH-357	SELF
Nov.	18	HUDSON	V-9169	SELF
Nov.	19	HUDSON	V-9129	SELF
Nov.	23	HUDSON	FH-332	SELF
Nov.	23	HUDSON	FH-331	SELF
Nov.	23	HUDSON	FH.332	SELF
Nov.	24	HUDSON	V-9392	SELF

OPERATIONAL TIME FOR NOVEMBER = 83.35

TOTAL OPERATIONAL TIME 2ND TOUR = 431.50

The
WEDGE IN
THE DOOR

Gibraltar 1942

EVERETT BAUDOUX

CONTACT:

Jane MacKay
P.O. Box 808
Dartmouth, NS
Canada B2Y 3Z3
jane@weareapt.com

ISBN 0-9781317-0-3

PHOTO CREDITS
All photographs are from the collection
of the author except for the following:

Keith Henderson's *A Bomber Flying Officer from Nova Scotia*
(Cover & Figure 2) is from the Beaverbrook Collection
of War Art, copyright the Canadian War Museum
(AN19710261-6085), and is used with permission.

The photo of the Beaufighter (Figure 8) is from the
Greenwood Military Aviation Museum Collection,
Greenwood, Nova Scotia, and is used with permission.

*The text of this book is typeset in
Jonathan Hoefler's Requiem types by Andrew Steeves &
printed offset under the direction of Gary Dunfield
at Gaspereau Press, Kentville, Nova Scotia.*

THIS BOOK IS DEDICATED TO THE
RAF 233 SQUADRON AIR AND GROUND CREWS

Although the maintenance and servicing personnel normally remained with the squadron for a year or more, the
air crew was constantly changing to replace casualties and
tour expired crews who had completed the maximum
hours operational time. Hence it is difficult to identify
individuals on squadron for more than a few months or in
specific circumstances. A further challenge with records
is that personnel from various countries and air forces
were seconded to RAF squadrons on a temporary basis; the
arrangement created a healthy cosmopolitan flavour in the
squadron identity. In RAF 233 GR Squadron the percentage
of RCAF Canadians was always a substantial number along
with British, Irish, Australian, New Zealand
and South African nationals.

I want to pay tribute to all those who served with RAF 233
Squadron at Gibraltar in those difficult months of 1942
when it was key to the Mediterranean and
North African Campaign.

Fortis et Fildelis · *Strong & faithful*

CONTENTS

April 16, 1942. Just after dawn we passed Point Tarifa on the southern tip of Spain, the Mediterranean spilling open before us, and there stood Gibraltar, its unmistakable rock formation one of the most recognizable pieces of geography in the world. Ahead of us, through the nine-mile gap of the Pillars of Hercules, lay waters and lands of astounding cultural achievement and of epic conflict somehow imprinted on this stony, independent bastion. Its very shape, like a half-submerged sea monster, stark in the early morning light, its western slopes shaded, a place of sharp opposing forces. Not a haven, I thought, and not foreboding. Implacable. Belonging to Gibraltar must take decades, generations.

Flying in with a navigator, a wireless op, and a gunner, I felt we were being recruited as guardians of this rock, to share its future in the struggles to come.

FIGURE I

Pilot Officer Baudoux flying an Anson pre-war in Scotland

AUTHOR'S PREFACE

This book describes the swift and risky establishment of vital air operations from the perspective of my own role in the first squadron of aircraft based at Gibraltar's tiny landing strip, which became the essential launching pad for the North African invasion: Operation TORCH.

Although the book contains specific chronological and statistical data of events, my main objective has been to portray the activity and spirit of the isolated military outpost of Gibraltar in 1942, and its crucial role in the Allied strategy for victory.

The 233 Squadron of Hudson aircraft flew shipping escort and anti-U-boat duties in circumstances made hazardous not only by enemy action but also by isolation from any alternative landing area: the nearest friendly airport was at RAF Portreath at the western tip of Cornwall, England—1,100 nautical miles and at least seven hours flying time, usually at night—or at Malta, another 1,100 miles to the east. For solitary aircraft, the missions demanded serious individual commitment; as a result of these solo missions, most aircraft crews who did not return were lost for reasons known neither then nor now, lost forever to some unknown engagement—perhaps weather, perhaps enemy activity, perhaps mechanical failure. In our eight months in Gibraltar leading up to the November 1942 invasion of North Africa, we know the causes of only five of twelve crews lost in operations.

There is no particular attempt to list specific actions or identify crews. All shouldered, equally, the workload and the risk.

EVERETT BAUDOUX
Big Island, Pictou County, Nova Scotia
August 2005

FIGURE 2
Everett Baudoux depicted in Keith Henderson's painting
A Bomber Flying Officer from Nova Scotia
(*Canadian War Museum*)

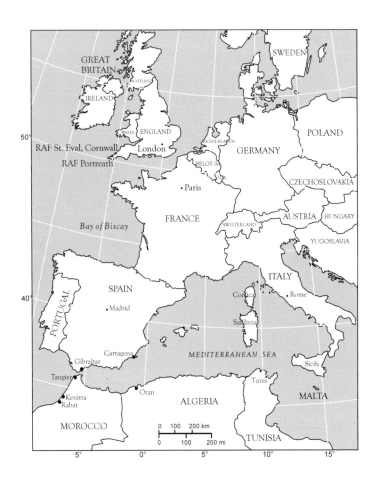

FIGURE 3

Gibraltar—1,100 nautical miles from the UK and 1,100 more to Malta

CHAPTER ONE

THE PILLAR OF HERCULES

In the war years of 1940–42, the future sovereignty of western governments and democratic values depended on the ability of the British Isles to ward off invasion and to counter U-boat attempts to sever its ocean lifelines. Britain and her allies desperately needed to retain a base from which to eventually launch an invasion that would deliver Europe from Nazi German occupation.

Several small pieces of land were of immense strategic importance, one of them just a massive wall of Jurassic-era limestone at the western entrance to the Mediterranean: Gibraltar.

Known as The Pillar of Hercules in Ancient Greece, as *Calpe* or *Alybe* to the Romans, this scrap of land we called the 'The Rock' had for centuries been besieged and occupied by Moorish, Spanish and British forces—a history that is etched in its own name. 'Gibraltar' comes from *jábal al Táriq*, or 'mount of Tariq', after the Moslem leader who, though vastly outnumbered, drove out the Spanish in A.D. 711. The Arabic *jábal* is related to the Hebrew *gebhûl*, originally 'earth wall or mountain serving as boundary': an apt description.

The Moors remained in almost continuous possession of Gibraltar for over seven hundred years. In 1462, Spain took possession once again, holding on until 1704, when their garrison was defeated by British naval forces. Although given the option of remaining on Gibraltar under British rule, all but one hundred Spanish left, an exodus that made room for the forebears of the current population: Genoese, Portuguese, and Moroccan Jews. That meld of race and cultures created a distinct Mediterranean people with British allegiance and a clear, independent identity as people of Gibraltar, speaking a distinct Spanish dialect along with the (official) English language.

The people of Gibraltar did not consider it an extension of Spain and denied any Spanish territorial claim—a claim formally relinquished by Treaty in 1713 but revived in later years, with Spain claiming historical rights. Although their position was ignored by Britain and by native Gibraltarians, Spain remained adamant and several times attempted to take the Rock. One such siege lasted three years (1779–1783); all ended in failure.

THE ROCK IN WORLD WAR TWO

Gibraltar's long and bitter history continued to play out in 1940, with the British, this time, in a precarious position. The fascist government of Spain's General Franco had received, in the recent civil war, some military help from Germany and now was disposed to be accommodating to Hitler, though not as a full Axis partner. Franco had good reason to sit on the fence. He knew the defensive resilience of Gibraltar; it was perhaps one of the most defendable fortresses in the world. Its sheltered gun emplacements high on the Rock put lower opposing artillery at a great disadvantage; moreover, the narrow isthmus connecting Spain to Gibraltar was mined and utterly exposed to defensive artillery fire; also Spanish colonial possessions were vulnerable to a British navy that would waste no time in taking retribution. Still impoverished by the recent civil war, attacking this fortress was not a gamble that Franco was prepared to take. The risk became even less acceptable when the United States joined the war against Germany. So the existing state of convenient tolerance continued in an arrangement of mutual, low-key, distrustful acceptance.

Local Spaniards were allowed to work in Gibraltar during daylight hours, with approximately two thousand travelling back and forth across the border each day. Most were women who worked in domestic and commercial support services, which had once been performed by some of the sixteen thousand Gibraltarian women and children evacuated in 1940–41 to the United Kingdom and to neutral ports of North Africa, for safer haven. With their absence, family life was suspended, replaced by the stark military atmosphere of a garrison at war.

After the surrender of France in 1940, and the eviction of all other Allied military forces from Europe, the only part of the continent remaining in Allied possession was the two-and-a-half miles of Gibraltar. Its importance as a guardian of the western entrance to the Mediterranean Sea and its symbolic invincibility were no longer metaphoric phrases: Gibraltar's survival as a fortress and as a naval base linked to all of the Near and Middle East was now essential to any real hope of reversing the disastrous course of war in the Mediterranean, North Africa, and southern Europe. For the British, the fortunes of war had fallen to a low, even precarious, point. Gibraltar was the only logical staging post for an invasion of enemy-occupied North Africa and, from there, Italy and other Mediterranean areas.

During this tense time in 1940–41, the British had reliable information that the Germans were negotiating with Spain to join them in the war against the Allies; this joint venture would allow Axis military passage through Spain for the capture of Gibraltar. To achieve its overall goals for this war, the logical strategy for Germany was to block access to the Mediterranean, choking off supplies to Malta, the direct route to Egypt and to the Middle East and thereby a route to India and the Far East. For this plan, Germany had prepared an operation, code-named "Felix," which would move the German 3rd Panzer Division through Spain to assault Gibraltar. But the proposal, spelled out by Hitler in a letter to General Franco, could create new problems with Vichy France and risk rupturing the armistice relationship that kept French Morocco and Algeria neutral. Moreover, several hundred thousand French troops in North Africa were non-belligerents, deterring any Allied occupation or an attempt by Spain, with Axis powers, to confiscate any French protectorate lands of North Africa. Hitler's thinking, seen in post-war documents, indicates that he was reluctant to enter Spain uninvited or on Franco's terms. And creating a breach in Vichy French neutrality would divert more of his already-dispersed military strength, which he needed for the Russian campaign.

Not all obstacles to his ambitions for Gibraltar were known to Hitler. One deterrent, for example, was disclosed only to top-level British security service (MI5) and Government leaders: there existed an anti-Hitler cadre made up of high-ranking German military officers dedicated to the overthrow of Hitler and the Nazi regime. This clandestine group, known amongst themselves as the *Schwarze Kapelle*, included some of the old-guard *Wehrmacht* senior army generals. They were convinced that the final outcome of the war would be disastrous to their country and saw it as their duty to frustrate the ego of an autocratic despot by obstructing his military plans through deceptive information and through his possible assassination.

A leader in this endeavour was none other than the head of the German secret service, *Abwehr* Admiral Wilhelm Canaris. He was neither a mole for the British nor a traitor in the service of an Allied nation; he was a deeply committed German patriot who was convinced that his country would be devastated by Hitler and his henchman. Canaris's plan was to instigate the Nazi downfall by skillful connivance. Germany directed him to discuss, with the Spanish government, an assault for the capture of Gibraltar, and to advise on military and political obstacles that the German panzer would encounter. Canaris, in collusion with a top-level advisor to Franco, prepared a clever, negative report, inventing additional deterrents, such as a need for large-calibre siege artillery not available in the German arsenal. In this particular scheme, Canaris's Spanish colleagues orchestrated Franco's dialogue with Hitler to delay and discourage Operation "Felix."

As with so many military ploys, this one came close to destruction in a proposed action by British MI5 agents in Gibraltar. They'd been made aware of Canaris's presence in the adjacent town of Algeciras—a main base for *Abwehr* German agents in Spain and only a scant five miles from Gibraltar, across the bay. MI5 planned to kidnap Canaris in Algeciras, a feat quite feasible. With the approval of Gibraltar's Governor, Lieutenant-General Mason-Macfarlane (whose concurrence with the kidnapping was mandatory) authorization of the project was requested from London. The Gibraltar agents, unaware of Canaris's clandestine activities within the German hierarchy, must have been more than a little puzzled when London did not approve.

Spanish misgivings about the consequence of a German alliance were indeed real; it was unlikely to help Franco get the territories he sought. His vacillations became tiresome to

Hitler, who was growing more preoccupied by the Russian conflict and who is reported to have said he'd rather have his teeth extracted than spend another afternoon with Franco. Operation Felix was abandoned. It may well have been one of Hitler's greatest strategic mistakes of the war. As for the patriot, Admiral Canaris, his role in a plot to assassinate Hitler was discovered in 1944. After a summary trial, he was executed by the Gestapo.

"THE WEDGE IN THE DOOR"

In the years prior to the November 1942 launching of the North African campaign, Operation TORCH, Gibraltar stood alone as "the wedge in the door"; its remoteness from friendly territory presented a difficult supply problem. Gibraltar is about 1,100 nautical miles by sea from England and there were also the small, isolated, heavily-bombed British islands of Malta 1,100 miles east of Gibraltar and only 60 miles south of enemy territory in Sicily. The limited resources of both Malta and Gibraltar left them dependent on merchant ships passing through waters adjacent to enemy zones of intense operation.

Naturally, any ships in transit were prime targets for German aircraft and U-boats. For the Allies, keeping cargoes arriving meant a priority commitment of air and surface forces for the protection of both naval and merchant vessels; it also meant the use of well-placed aircraft and versatile crew trained in maritime operations. Ergo, justification for the top-priority construction of an air base at Gibraltar was obvious. A significant portion of the initial anti-submarine and air escort duty was delegated to Catalina flying boat squadrons of the Royal Air Force. They operated from the

400-acre Gibraltar Harbour, enclosed by concrete walls known as "sea moles," which formed protective barriers. Although these aircraft performed sterling service over the Atlantic, they were slow and vulnerable to U-boat gunfire. And in areas where they encountered enemy aircraft with superior fighting capability, their ability to survive was less than marginal.

Clearly, the Allies needed a facility for land-based aircraft, not only to bolster and add strength for escort and anti-U-boat operations but also to establish a reliable air link between the United Kingdom (UK) and Gibraltar and onward transit to the Middle East. There could be no less likely sites for an airfield than Gibraltar. Any thoughts of constructing a separate landing strip or runway in the waters adjoining the Rock were fraught with enormous difficulties and considered out of the question. Thus, the only flat surface that had any possibility for airfield or runway was the area of the horse race track on the isthmus connecting to Spain.

FROM RACECOURSE TO RUNWAY

The towering north front rock of Gibraltar rose to a height of 1,400 feet above a 1,000-foot-long racecourse. On the west end of the runway, the neutral zone and Spanish border was within two thousand feet, while the eastern end of the runway was within two hundred feet of the neutral zone barrier. These limitations defined the land area available without violation of the agreed border. A landing strip could only run east-west, over the racecourse, thus operating in the limited space in wind would be much like landing on an aircraft carrier; the initial length was about 2,700 feet with water at either end.

War demands bold decisions; officials in Air Ministry said "do it" and the army engineers made haste to comply. The urgency of deploying land-based aircraft to Gibraltar drove the decision to commence operations immediately with the minimum possible landing strip. In December 1941, 233 Squadron dispatched three aircraft from RAF St. Evel in Cornwall to Gibraltar North Front. By February 1942, the number was eight Hudsons, then sixteen. They commenced full operations along with 202 and 210 flying boat squadrons and several Royal Navy Swordfish biplanes. Their enormous task was to provide protective cover in the Atlantic and Mediterranean Seas east and west of Gibraltar, where U-boat attacks were crippling Allied merchant marine and navy shipping. By June 1942, a 3,200-foot runway was inching its way into Algeciras Bay (also known as the Bay of Gibraltar, or simply the Bay, this large, sweeping bay is shared by Spain and the British territory of Gibraltar). The air war from Gibraltar was established but it would be another five months before additional help joined 233 squadron at North Front with the arrival of 500, 48, and 608 Squadrons in October and November 1942. Meanwhile, hundreds of aircraft of all types would arrive at Gibraltar for onward transit to Malta, Egypt and the Far East. The marshalling of fighters, bombers, and transports to launch the invasions of North Africa in November 1942 and Southern France 1944 was our twentieth-century version of the myth of the Pillar of Hercules. The invasions proved effective and most military historians agree that the effect of the campaigns in diverting strong, experienced elements of the German forces to Africa and Italy contributed to the success of the cross-channel D-Day invasion of France by Allied forces. And we now know that the experience gained in the coordination of massive forces in the North African invasion was a major factor in the success of the 1944–45 European campaign. But in the tense, dangerous months of 1942, Gibraltar's fate was uncertain and its war demanded and extracted the utmost human resolve, both in the air and on the ground.

JANUARY 1942:
EARLY FLIGHTS AT GIBRALTAR[†]

Frequent and unexpected bad weather with the resulting turbulence off a towering 1,400-foot wall of rock within 2,500 feet of the runway meant landing was a challenge. The single 3,000-foot runway gave no quarter in a cross wind, in rain, at night ... In the first ten months of 1942, Gibraltar's landing strip was unforgiving of anything less than sharp, precise piloting. Even with that, weather was always out of our control and often unpredictable, creating many critical incidents for myself and others—such as Flying Officer Jim Kennedy's unlucky January 13 landing attempt:

> We were briefed with two or three other crews to do an A/S sweep west. There was a shortage of Syco coding cards, and we were given one from the previous period. I asked the Controller to please remember this when sending us any messages.
>
> The met. forecast was for overcast about 1500' and a risk of showers out in the Atlantic. We were airborne mid-to-late afternoon and proceeded through the Strait. The weather started to close in as we flew west. The ceiling lowered and the wind increased. At some

---

[†] Some material in this section is attributed to Jim Kennedy and comes from personal letters and phone calls between the author and Kennedy (who lives in Victoria, British Columbia) in preparation for this book. This material, where used, has not been altered by the author and retains Kennedy's original phrasing.

time between 2 and 3 hours, Sergeant Morley told me he'd received a signal, addressed to us and other A/C on the sweep, which he could not decipher. He had asked for a repeat and got the same signal. It was obvious that they'd forgotten the odd Syco. I told him to send, in plain language, that we could not understand [their signal]. They came back with an immediate recall in plain language. The weather had closed in at base. By this time we were almost on deck, the visibility was poor, and it was getting dark.

John gave me a course for the Strait (he was a good navigator). As the Strait were narrow, our chances of missing land on both sides and flying through were iffy. We had to stay below the overcast to pick up a landfall, as this was the only safe way to get home. A landfall at our altitude under those conditions would be hairy. We had the ASV [radar] on and all hands watching for surf.

We flew like this with both the small windows open and the rain coming in, and suddenly the surf was right under us. We just cleared the lighthouse at Cape Spartel. Then the glow from the lights of Tangier lit up the overcast. John had a course ready for us to go through the Strait. Visibility was just about zero and black as the inside of a cow. By this time we were talking to Gibraltar, and I asked for lights to help us find the Rock. The searchlights were turned on, and we could just see the glow. We flew well past what we thought was Europe Point and turned left for an east-to-west approach. John was sitting on the top of the steps beside me when we hit a great bloody down-draft. It dropped us almost into the drink, and John ended up on his hands and knees down in the nose.

We found the end of the runway, carried on along the coast, and turned for our approach, but we could see the flarepath only when we were directly over it. We tried several times to approach and land, without success. Also, we were being bounced around violently on each approach; Morley [sic] and Moore were trying to hide under the bunk to avoid the flying objects—camera, parachutes, etc.

Finally I gave up and flew into Algeciras [sic] Bay, where it was at least less turbulent. Got permission to try landing downwind. It was given reluctantly and, after a number of attempts, we made it.

Tich Maudsley was the first one into the A/C, where we stopped in the dispersal. He said that Dad (Devey) had ordered the recall when he saw how the weather was deteriorating and that he got into a chewing match with the met. man at Europe over his lousy forecasting. And that turkey said the lousy conditions were local at North Front!

The poor conditions that January day caused another 233 Squadron aircraft, with a less experienced pilot, to be "trapped out". The pilot's account describes the hazardous conditions at Gibraltar that would greet me upon my own arrival a few weeks later:

... flying 'H' (AM 564) on another anti-submarine patrol down the African coast, we received a call to return to base as the weather was closing in. By the time we got back, the Rock was covered in mist, a gale was blowing, visibility restricted by pouring rain. I made two attempts at normal landing but at 'hold off' position, with the undercarriage lowered, the aircraft buffeted by the swirl and eddies caused by the gusty wind blowing round the Rock. The aircraft became unmanageable, so—retracting the undercarriage—I overshot and flew up into the overcast. After the second unsuccessful attempt, I dropped my load of depth charges into the Mediterranean Sea. The aircraft stalled but I managed to recover just in time to see the white horses on the surface of the sea. The instruments were going crazy, but by flying the plane by the seat of my pants, as they

say, I turned away from the Rock. I came in to land for
the third time, determined to get down. The crew were
ordered to go aft and prepare for a crash landing. I belly
landed without lowering the undercarriage, wrecking
the propellers and skidding to a halt, [saving the crew
but] writing off a valuable aircraft.

In these months before TORCH and the Allied occupation of North Africa, the absence of any alternative airfield
within fuel range for land-based aircraft lent extra hazard
to all our flights and made for some seat-of-the-pants solutions. Flight Lieutenant Jim Kennedy joined 233 Squadron
at St. Eval in early November 1941, crewing up with Flying
Officer Paul Scott:

We did A/S sweeps over the Bay of Biscay until late
that month, when the squadron was ordered to provide
several aircraft to operate from Gibraltar. For some
time after our arrival at the Rock, our pre-flight and
post-flight briefing was done from the flying boat base
Operations Room as there was no ops room at North
Front. I flew with Paul Scott and Dad Devey until
January 3, 1942, and was made Captain on January 4.

Kennedy's experience in 233 Squadron gives a clear picture
of flying operations at Gibraltar in the months and weeks
preceding my own mid-April arrival:

On April 5 we were briefed to do a recce of Casablanca
harbour to check on the French fleet based there. We
were to use our own discretion on how we would do
this. My crew at that time were FO Graham Taylor
observer, PO Frank Lewis W/Op. and Sgt. Frank Ash
W/Op. We were airborne mid-afternoon, and I decided
that it would be safer to approach from inland—more

of a surprise and a better chance to count ships. We turned inland south of Rabat and flew south along the foothills to just east of Casablanca, then turned west and flew over the city and the harbour. We were down pretty low and caused a lot of excitement. Each one of us had a job—I was to count battleships, as there would not be too many of them and I'd be busy anyway. Graham [Taylor] was to count cruisers, [Frank] Lewis to count destroyers and Frank [Ash] was to look for submarines. There were people running in all directions, and the matelots with their red pompoms running along the deck of the Jean Bart (I think). We also saw a huge tidal swimming pool on the beach, and in all the panic we were causing our count was not complete.

We had to do it all over again. This time, they were semi-ready for us. We were over the harbour with our count complete and out to sea when they opened up—not very effectively. (A couple of weeks later, Pilot Officer Tommy Masters and crew were to fly along the coast of Casablanca and not go too close. He was a few miles off Casablanca when a flight of French Dewoitine fighters came up alongside them, fell back behind him, and one opened up, wounding the navigator in the legs.)

[Later that year] We were flying escort to a convoy and its naval escort, headed east. Somewhere east of Cape De Gata, we received a recall. To acknowledge, I flew south and east about thirty miles to reply. When I tried to engage the auto-pilot, it would not work. I checked the servo oil pressure: there was none, so the undercarriage and flaps would not operate.

I ordered the crew to urinate in their thermos bottles. Later, when we were approaching the Rock, I tried to lower the undercarriage without success. Frank Ash removed the W/Op's seat from in front of the Servo tank. Then, using a heavy Admiralty chart as a funnel, Reggie and Frank poured the piss into the servo. With a few hand pumps, the pressure on the gauge went up, and I lowered the undercarriage and the flaps.

After landing, I told Chief Hudson (a good head) what we had done. He was not impressed. "In the heat, who is going to want to do the service?"

Crew remarks:

"It was easier but less noble than giving blood."

"We were called on to give all we had and the crew was drained to save the ship."

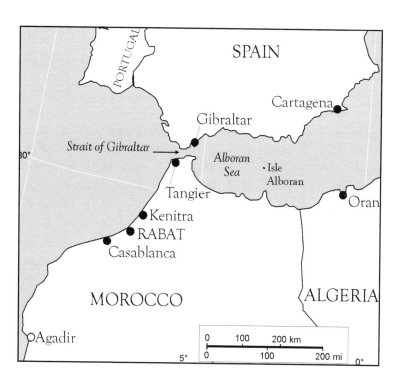

FIGURE 4
The theater of operations around Gibraltar

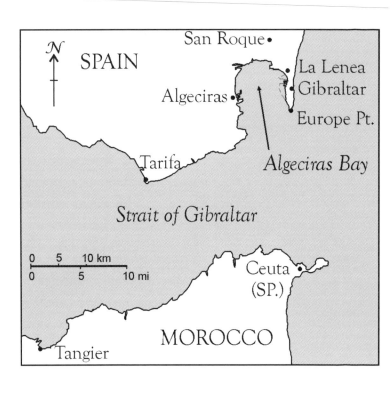

FIGURE 5
The Strait of Gibraltar

CHAPTER TWO

NEW ORDERS

March 27, 1942: Squadron Leader Dennis Spotswood, the Officer Commanding "B" Flight at Number 6 Operational Training Unit (OTU), gave me the welcome news that I was posted back to operational duty with my old squadron. I'd spent most of 1940 with 233 Squadron flying Hudsons from RAF Leuchars in Scotland, a tough year of operations—long-range fighter cover against German bombers, shipping strikes from Denmark to northern Norway, and bombing raids on Norwegian targets, as well as routine anti-submarine patrols and reconnaissance. We'd been heavily involved in the attempt to prevent the invasion of Norway, but in the end this wasn't within the Allies' military resources. Many of my companions had not survived the year; somehow, I'd come through 420 flying hours of operations and earned a Distinguished Flying Cross. Now, with improved flying skills, experience, and whatever luck I had left, my performance—and chance of survival—should be better.

Although the new posting brought with it a promotion to Squadron Leader, I wasn't pleased at the prospect of continuing on the Hudson aircraft for another tour of operations. I didn't lack confidence in the Hudson; I didn't doubt my ability to handle the machine with skill; but I wanted to go to a Beaufighter night-fighter squadron and had managed to qualify for such a posting by arranging a full Beaufighter conversion. Dennis (later Marshal of the Royal Air Force Sir Dennis Spotswood) had done me a special favour, as he worked with a man who happened to be the Officer Commanding (OC) of the Beaufighter Operational Training Unit at RAF Catfoss. A high percentage of my own flying had been at night, and I was equally comfortable piloting at night as by day; I saw it as a new challenge. But it was not to be. "Theirs is not to reason why: theirs is but to do or die," as Tennyson says. War is never rational.

Four days later I was at RAF Portreath in Cornwall, reporting to Squadron Commander Terry McComb who, like I, was a recycled 233 Squadron pilot of 1939–40. Our old 233 Squadron was split into two flights, with the OC and "A" flight at Portreath and the "B" flight recently sent to Gibraltar on shipping protection and anti-submarine duties. I was second in command of 233 and now would be taking over the Gibraltar operation. And so, on the night of April 16, 1942, with a new crew of sergeant navigator, sergeant wireless op, and sergeant gunner, aircraft AM 537 took off for Gibraltar.

A LONG JOURNEY

At times it struck me—here I was, Ev Baudoux from Stellarton, Nova Scotia, flying a technically modern aircraft en route to a destination that had played such a historic role in both culture and conflict. As we flew through the night, it seemed incredible that my ambition to be an aviator had gone from intention to reality in less than four years.

Back in Pictou County—small towns surrounded by coal seams, rural farmland, and the sea—my own father was a mine manager, though he'd taken a two-year correspondence course in aviation engineering, just for interest. It was he who brought me, five years old, to see United States Navy sea planes land in Pictou Harbour on their round-the-world tour. From that moment my need to fly took root, and this fixation on a career in aviation never wavered. My schoolbooks were filled with drawings of airplanes, and the sound of an approaching aircraft motor would have me on my bicycle pedalling furiously for the airfield. At seventeen, this single-mindedness had me in the cockpit of an Avro Avian and Gypsy Moth at nearby Trenton Airfield, and I soon earned a private pilot's licence there.

But even my intense ambition couldn't change the times: it was the late 1930s, and continuing economic depression made the step from pilot's licence to viable career almost beyond possibility. I wrote to many commercial and industrial aviation operations, offering to work for keep and for experience, to no avail. Finally, I contacted the Royal Canadian Air Force (RCAF) in Halifax, Nova Scotia, where I went through a screening process of physical and written exams and interviews. I passed the entry test, but official acceptance and entry to training would likely take another eighteen to twenty-four months. To me that was unacceptable. I learned that if an RCAF final interview board in Ottawa confirmed my suitability, the British Royal Air Force (RAF) would pay my way to the United Kingdom, where I could start basic training immediately. If that training was successful, I'd be given advanced pilot training and a commission in the RAF as an Acting Pilot Officer.

I took the train from Stellarton to Ottawa for an interview by the RAF selection board. (The board was chaired by Squadron Leader Slemon, who would later become an air marshal as Chief of Staff). There, I discovered that I was one of about eighteen applicants selected from across Canada; I presented my credentials and my letters of reference, and after twenty minutes giving answers and explanations, I was told to report back to headquarters at three o'clock that same afternoon.

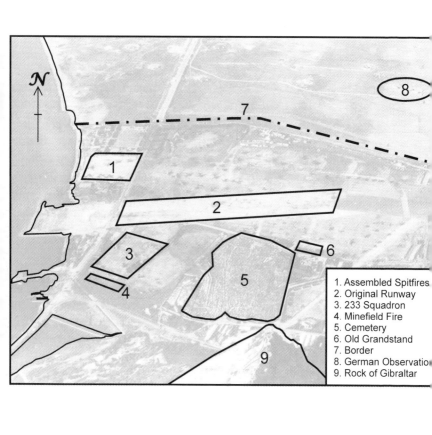

1. Assembled Spitfires
2. Original Runway
3. 233 Squadron
4. Minefield Fire
5. Cemetery
6. Old Grandstand
7. Border
8. German Observation
9. Rock of Gibraltar

FIGURE 6

The 3,000 foot runway was squeezed by the Spanish boarder on the north and the 1,400 foot 'rock' on the south. (Key on facing page.)

Punctually at three I was ushered into an office, "You've been accepted," I was told. "Here are your tickets to Saint John, New Brunswick, on this evening's train, and on the *Duchess of York*, which sails for Scotland tomorrow." There was also some cash for expenses; the tickets were for first class.

When I boarded the train that evening I found that eight others, mostly from the western provinces, had also been accepted. Examining the ship ticket, I noticed it showed a stopover of a few hours in Halifax. This was lucky, as my small travelling luggage for a three-day trip to Ottawa didn't seem adequate for the adventure now before me – two years would pass before a return home on leave. A phone call brought my father and brother to Halifax with extra clothes and cash and *bon voyage*. By the time the Duchess of York docked a week later in Greenock, Scotland, my eight fellow travellers and I had moved from companions to friends. Only three of us would survive the coming war. Arriving in Scotland, we went to Scone, near Perth, to fly Tiger Moths at the civilian training school; I managed to get an above-average pilot rating and an RAF commission in 1939. War clouds loomed.

And now, I thought, we flew through the April night to one of the most fought-over pieces of turf in the middle of a seemingly endless conflict. Briefings on operations at Gibraltar had been skimpy, though brevity of information wasn't unusual as it was a new airstrip still under construction, and experience on flight operations there could be measured in weeks, rather than months or years.

We approached the Strait from the west in the early morning. Just after dawn we passed Point Tarifa on the southern tip of Spain, the Mediterranean spilling open before us, and there stood Gibraltar, its unmistakable rock formation one of the most recognizable pieces of geography in the world.

Ahead of us, through the nine-mile gap of the Pillars of Hercules, lay waters and lands of astounding cultural achievement and epic conflict, all somehow imprinted on this stony, independent bastion. Its very shape, like a half-submerged sea monster, stark in the early morning light, its western slopes shaded—a place of sharp opposing forces. Not a haven, I felt, and not foreboding. Implacable. Belonging to Gibraltar must take decades, or generations.

WELCOME TO GIBRALTAR

I thought of mythological Gibraltar, known to ancient Greeks and Romans as *Calpe* or *Alybe*. I thought, too, of the long and violent politics played out here, testament to human folly, and how we now followed in that flawed pursuit in our own modern metal Pegasus. But the work at hand: Cape Trafalgar and Tarifa on the port side, then directly to Gibraltar Europa Point; we flash the recognition signal of the day and proceed down the Bay of Gibraltar to the North Front air strip.

And a strip it was. The runway protruded about four hundred feet into the Bay, where men with vehicles were dumping and compacting rock fill, still extending it into the bay. A radioed clearance to land came from the improvised control "tower" mounted atop the old racecourse building. As we approached, airstrip workers quickly moved to the sides of the construction, going back to work as soon as we'd passed for touchdown. Clearly, this was a top priority job with no time to waste.

The small airfield of about 140 acres looked makeshift, devoid of any orderly or impressive structures, the whole place cobbled together, using whatever was at hand. Vestiges of the racecourse buildings that once housed animals now held offices and aviation equipment. Small patches of remaining vegetation only emphasized the drab, utilitarian surround. The only significant relief came from cultivated flowering plants in the cemetery, safely enclosed by the customary high masonry wall of Iberian burial grounds; its location on the isthmus most likely chosen for the loose sand not found elsewhere on the Rock.

The grandstand of the former oval track was the largest concrete building with some modest "clubhouse" accommodation. A strip of ground about 150 feet wide ran parallel to the 300-foot-breadth of the runway, serving as aircraft taxi way and a road for service vehicles. Land on the north of the runway was used mainly for aircraft dispersal and storage. When racecourse became airstrip, open space was important and obstructive buildings had to come down. One exception stood near the north-east barrier of the neutral ground, a modest house kept for the station commander's residence. The rest of us weren't so fortunate.

Living quarters for all ranks couldn't accommodate even the small increase in personnel for our squadron and ground crews. During the first five months at Gibraltar, most crews billeted in the two main hotels. Sleeping and messing facilities weren't the only shortage; inadequate toilets and ablutions were ancient and not up to the standards that climate and dust made essential for general health. But comfort was a low priority—basic, functional utilities were the standard here. Steel Nissen huts and other speedily assembled structures mushroomed; the packing crates that had contained Spitfire fighters as ship cargo now were converted to accommodation. When living quarters did become available at North Front, they were the least desirable on Gibraltar, particularly in the hot summer months.

I wasn't the only one to be struck by all this upon arrival. Jim Kennedy (Flying Officer) arrived at Gibraltar in 1941:

> The officers were billeted at the Bristol Hotel and all of us shared one room. As I remember, there were Hugh ('Dad') Devey, Tich Maudsley, John Wilson, Paul Scott, Ernie Corken and myself. More were to follow. By the time the shaving water got down to the junior bog-rat (me), it had skim on it thicker than icing on a Christmas cake.
>
> As rooms became available, they were occupied in descending order of rank. There was never an empty bed in the room as each one was filled immediately by escapees from Europe (Czechs, Poles Dutch). We stayed at the hotel until (I think) the following June...Then we were moved to North Front and lived in Spitfire packing cases which leaked like sieves when it rained. The twice-daily blasting of the slag pile at the face of the Rock knocked a few holes in our homes. Shortly after this, we moved into rooms on the viewers' side of the grandstand. It was odd going down steps to get into your bunk.

Comments from ground crews and aircrew arriving at Gibraltar all carry the same impression of crude, inadequate facilities—even from those used to the improvisation of war.

> We settled down to sleep in Nissen huts on the cases which had contained the fuel for use on the aircraft, later changed for the normal type of iron beds. We made friends with an anti-aircraft unit which had been there for the whole duration of the war. They had no comforts of any sort, but by the time we left, they were provided with RAF sheets and tablecloths.

We spent a very pleasant Christmas with them, watching from a hole high up in the face of the Rock, the soldiers heaving loads of chalk and other debris from their tunnellings through the rock, and some Wimpeys (Wellingtons) bound for Malta, piloted by fellows straight from Operational Training Unit (OTU) overshoot the short runway and plunge into the sea.

The tiny runway and the scant living quarters were still more bearable than the seasonal absence of fresh water for showering or dressing. Conservation of rainwater in interior reservoirs made it necessary to pump salt water into the lines for all ablution uses. Military-issue saltwater soap was no substitute for the freshwater variety; after three months, we were convinced that prolonged use would eventually encase our bodies in permanent layers of marine sediment.

The only freshwater well that seemed to remain in continuous use was ancient and lay in the ruins of the old Moor castle. Here, close to the isthmus sand formation, the ancient well supplied laundry water for the Spanish women who ran the daily out-of-doors service. It appeared to be for their exclusive use and was probably unpotable. The squadron medical officer warned us not to drink water from other-than-approved sources nor eat unwashed fruit; the unhappy result of ignoring this advice was a debilitating attack of the "Gib scours."

Local residents handled the seasonal shortage with rainwater catchments and storage cisterns. Hotels, in particular, had significant internal supplementary reservoirs. But in periods of long drought, from May to October, it sometimes became necessary to import tanker ships of water. And Gibraltar's escalating water needs exceeded the capacity of the massive eastern slope catchment area and internal storage system.

Eventually, in late 1943 the problem was resolved by installing equipment to convert sea water; the market for saltwater soap was then in merciful decline.

Perhaps the lack of comfort, the crude environment, and the daily minor annoyances had a pioneering effect, focussing our resolve and our attention to the work we'd been sent there to do. Duress in moderation is a motivating spur to get on with the job, and that we did. On the three days following our arrival at Gibraltar, I flew successful patrols on convoy and navy ship protection. This was no time for moping, no time for trivial concerns.

CHAPTER THREE

SAPPERS AT GIBRALTAR

British War Office strategists knew that the fate of Gibraltar in World War Two could predict the course of the war and subsequent history. Gibraltar was the gateway to the Mediterranean sea route for Allied shipping; the tiny British colony also was essential for support of land and sea forces fighting to retain possession of Egypt, the Suez Canal, and Allied territory east of the Suez. A strong position in Gibraltar made it possible to strengthen Allied forces in Malta, which would restrict shipping supplies to enemy formations in the African conflict.

The strategic implications were clear: without Malta, the central basin of the Mediterranean would be an unhindered supply route for the German North African Army Corps; without Gibraltar, Malta could not be provisioned, which would make inevitable a domino collapse of the Allied position.

ROYAL CANADIAN ENGINEERS
NO. I TUNNELLING COMPANY

Prior to 1940, Gibraltar had been neglected, but it now became a top-priority commitment for military construction; it badly needed an aircraft runway and upgraded defences, as well as appropriate facilities to support these. The tunnelling engineering unit at Gibraltar was woefully inadequate for the massive task that lay before it, and there were no reserves available in the UK forces to give Gibraltar additional support. On October 23, 1940, the UK Secretary of State for Dominion Affairs, Lord Cranborne, addressed an urgent appeal to Vincent Massey, the Canadian High Commissioner in London, asking that the England-based No.1 Tunnelling Company of the Royal Canadian Engineers (RCE) send a unit to Gibraltar. Massey quickly approved the measure, and by late November this Company was excavating new installations within the Rock. In February 1942, a second Special Detachment of the RCE No.1 Tunnelling Company arrived to extend the 3,000-foot runway another 2,400 feet into the Bay of Gibraltar. The decision to allocate this task to experienced hard-rock miners from Canada was fortuitous.

These experienced professionals were in their element and wasted no time in excavating the material needed for runway fill, using new and superior methods. Limestone scree needed to be excavated from a large mound at the base of the north face of the Rock, and—before the Canadians took over this task—drilling and blasting had been the standard technique. This compacted material had accumulated over thousands of years of flaking from the north face of the Rock and had a concrete-like consistency; dislodging it with explosives was not only tedious but dangerous, with debris flying near the airfield installations. When the engineers were about to ignite a blasting charge, they gave a warning five minutes prior to the explosion: a loud claxton sounded a short series of hoots. All persons within a thousand yards took cover behind masonry walls or in steel Nissen huts while chunks of material, some the size of grapefruit, rained down. This was no casual precaution; a stone missile killed one unfortunate officer who ventured outside the Officers' Mess.

The Canadians quickly introduced a high-pressure water hydraulic blasting system to loosen the scree. Large water pumps forced water through gun-like nozzles that then drained the water from the material back into the Bay through pipes and ditches. Construction was continuous, and the visible lengthening of the runway became a symbol of challenge, determination, and success. As the engineers worked non-stop, flying continued; if aircraft landing in an east-to-west direction failed to stop before tumbling into the mounds and pits of construction rubble, they simply became part of the buried structure. While the crews survived, those aircraft were not recovered.

RCE OFFICER COMMANDING:
MAJOR JACK TATHAM

Even as runway construction proceeded at full speed, the RCE had other tasks—excavating inside the Rock for a hospital (eventually Gort's Hospital) and its supporting facilities, creating additional water reservoirs and ammunition magazines, and building more access tunnels to the east face. The natural caves and caverns that they encountered in their work were used to hold materials from other excavations, reshaping forever this geologic landmark.

I became friends with the RCE's Officer Commanding, Major Jack Tatham. Jack was a robust six-footer in his early thirties with the direct, authoritative manner of a person used to getting things done. Once having made up his mind, Jack had little patience for delays or trivial detail. Once, after we'd become well acquainted, I chided him about his compulsion to make quick, on-the-spot decisions even when there was no press for speed. He told me that this worked well for him and gave, as example, a visit he'd made to a friend's family for the first time. He'd spent a couple of hours one afternoon getting to know his friend's sister, and before leaving, he told her they should marry before the end of the summer. While I don't know this woman's reaction to such audacity, I do know that theirs was a good, life-long commitment.

Jack was not a regular-force army officer but came from the same working environment as most (if not all) sappers in the unit. These war-time volunteers may have been clothed in military garb, but beneath that veneer lay the hard, practical attitude of Canadian miners. Discipline was functional and practical; professional conduct on the work site was expected and delivered. Hard work gave way to hard play, and the sappers' off-duty hours saw more than their fair share of altercations at Gibraltar's two licensed taverns. Garrison-town atmosphere and regulations were not particularly suited to their experience of mining-town life. Fortunately, Jack Tatham had the right measure of his men. They gave him their full support, and he was quick to intercede on their behalf if some unruly behaviour got more punishment than he thought necessary. Everyone in the tunnelling unit knew that Tatham's direction was not soft nor to be taken lightly. And in a place as confined as Gibraltar, the reputation of authority figures soon seeped out and became part of local, general knowledge. When a beer-fuelled fracas resulted in the Military Police carting off some of his troops to the local lock-up—with the business-like unbiased approach they showed all boisterous offenders—Tatham's policy was equally pragmatic. He never allowed his sappers to rest their hangovers in the detention centre when they could speed removal of tunnel rock with some extra-duty recovery therapy.

On a rare day off from squadron duty, I was visiting Jack and his officers, accompanying Tatham's duty officer on the afternoon rounds of the working sites. (In this way, I was able to see a great deal of the excavation work.) Duty officer Captain DeMorest was a forty-year-old sweat from the Sudbury region of Ontario; in civvy street, he was a diamond-drill crew captain who'd joined the army, continuing his profession with the added challenge and risk of war-time life. As DeMorest and I drove into the area where the future Gort's Hospital was in progress, the staff sergeant, with the captain, approached a busy, sweating group of sappers, produced a clipboard from under his arm, and called out "Private D———,[†] come forward."

I knew that during this inspection of sites some brief, routine administration would occur. Still, I was surprised that the 'admin' matter concerned the hearing and summary judgement of miscreants charged with various inebriation offences. Here, there was no production time lost in orderly parades and ritual—this was real frontier stuff. When the offender was ordered to step forward, the remaining crew stopped only for a moment, to adjust for his absence in the crew system, and even this pause brought a bellow from Captain DeMorest:

"Don't stop! Keep working!" Next came his question for the accused, now having a short rest from his labour: "How do you plead to the charge of being drunk and disorderly?"

"Guilty, sir."

"Fifteen-dollar fine and forty-eight hours confined to camp—get back to work."

[†]   Name not known.

With tongue in cheek, I was going to ask the captain how onerous could a two-day-confinement to camp on Gibraltar actually be. DeMorest must have read my mind. "You have to be strict about these things!"

THE TUNNELLERS' MESS AND THE PEACOCK

The following Sunday, I was treated to a respite from the dining fare of North Front mess by having supper with the engineers; their mess was three or four terraces up the west side, above the Rock Hotel, a pleasant villa with a walled garden that overlooked lower terraces and the bay of Gibraltar. While we were sitting in the peaceful isolation of the garden having our after-dinner coffee, a mess orderly approached Captain DeMorest with a message: Could the captain take a minute to see Private Ray MacDonald at the front entrance for an equipment voucher approval? When DeMorest left, the lieutenant sitting alongside me chuckled. "He fines the guys on his crew for drunkenness, then they come to borrow beer money from him when they're broke." I neglected to mention that I knew "Big" Ray MacDonald; he was from my own hometown of Stellarton, Nova Scotia.

The Tunnelling Engineers Mess, in contrast to my regular mess, was a different world. My military service in the RAF had started as a pre-war commissioned pilot officer stationed at airfields with messes that could hold a hundred or more members. Although mess life saw many friendships and unit affiliations, the number of members and the natural macho environment of an all-male residence required a firm, regulated code of behaviour. With the outbreak of war, this all-male protocol suffered a shock of instant reform with the inclusion of female officers into previously male-only mess sanctuaries. At RAF North Front, our mess had none of the club formalities or amenities of more established stations; there were no females, and the large number of transients seemed impervious to traditional graces or to squadron attachments. The war priority was clear, and the mess was just a fly-filled place to have a beer and some drab food. Strangely, we felt neither deprived nor depressed. Although our involvement in the war was not soft and was far from casualty-free, we were aware that, in Malta and in the desert fighting, all niceties of life had ceased to exist; this was neither the time nor the place for pre-war customs and social graces.

Yet less than two miles away, the Tunnelling Engineers Mess had an air of unity and civility, a family-like atmosphere. And for me at Gibraltar in 1942, this small sappers' mess was an oasis. When the supper meal was served, we all sat down with Jack Tatham at the head of the table, a kind of father of this family. He then requested one of the officers to say grace before we ate. The meal we shared was an hour of humanity, of value for individuals and for their collective commitment.

Although, during my own brief visits, the Tunnellers Officers Mess seemed a haven of tranquillity, its regular members made the frequent acquaintance of one noisy, raucous co-habitant of their sanctuary. This irritating fellow was a fixed resident with legal and contractual rights that prohibited his forceful restraint or eviction. Anyone who has lived near a bachelor peacock will know that this creature can give lessons in obnoxious tirade. From pre-dawn to sundown he shrieks continual complaint in loud, nerve-grating squawks and cries that cease only when he's resting his pipes for the next day's abuse. Gibraltar's peacocks, of course, were protected. But after one of his usual long and stressful days, Major Tatham's tolerance collapsed. He delegated a duty to the two most junior officers:

"I'll give you one week to get rid of the damned peacock, without exposing us to the authorities."

The problem was not simple, even for the ingenuity of first lieutenants. Rumour had it they tried to negotiate with other property owners to keep the bird as a paying boarder. That idea failed because—in the opinion of older hands—the young Canadians didn't have the negotiating skills to cut an acceptable deal with the native Gibraltarians. Their next solution was a stroke of pure opportunism. Governor Mason-Macfarlane had just honoured the RCE No.1 Tunnelling Company by presenting them with the symbol of the Keys, a singular recognition of their outstanding service to Gibraltar. The sappers responded with a scheme to rid themselves of a squawking bird. They prepared a flowery document, telling Governor Mason-Macfarlane that the Canadian Tunnellers would like to express their humble appreciation of the honour he had bestowed on them and leave an appropriate memento to grace the governor's garden: the gift of a gorgeous peacock.

Their scheme seemed to work; the gift was accepted, with a date of transfer and a little presentation ceremony arranged. The plan of these conniving sappers, though, had proceeded in the absence of the governor's regular aide-de-camp, who'd been away on detached duty. On his return, their good fortune collapsed; this aide was an old pro who knew all about peacocks, and he was able to convince the governor that certain rare botanical species in the garden could not co-exist with a peacock—terribly sorry....

Simple luck, on occasion, overcomes the worst adversity. And when the best-laid plans for peacock banishment failed, a wartime shortage of fresh eggs inspired a neighbour on a lower terrace to acquire from Spain a half-dozen hens to occupy his walled garden. The peacock took immediate notice of this potential harem and emigrated to the new site. (Peacocks must know the old truism about "a bird in the hand"....) I never did know if a new species of fowl appeared in Gibraltar gardens. Engineers, aside from being skillful, are sometimes lucky.

As for the Canadian engineers' generous invitations to dine in their civilized mess, my only way of reciprocating this kindness was to take a few people on local flights or on routine, ship-escort duty. But carrying an extra person on any operational flight was never a casual practice, particularly if the passenger was unfamiliar with air crew procedures and equipment. Additional briefing and care had to be detailed, an added responsibility for one or two crew, and no operation could be considered safe from enemy encounter. Still, several engineers were keen to experience an operational flight and gladly sacrificed a rare day off to make the trip. For obvious reasons, this was not a common practice.

THE KEEPER OF THE KEYS

While sappers at Gibraltar weren't exposed to any direct enemy action, the usual role of the engineering troops in combat situations was one of the most hazardous in military fighting. Their time and tasks here kept them away from front-line fire only until a new duty assignment called them back. Already well acquainted with danger in their peacetime occupation, these men had served as front-line soldiers in reconnaissance, assault preparation, bridge building, land-mine clearing, and other essential functions—often under heavy enemy fire. The history of the RCE units in the 1943 campaign in Italy and again in Belgium and Holland is one of outstanding gallantry. Aside from my brother Stirling, who served as a RCE sapper in both campaigns, Major R.B. Cameron, also from my home county of Pictou, Nova Scotia, was awarded the Distinguished Service Order (DSO) for outstanding courageous duty with the RCEs in Italy. My account of the Tunnelling Company's duties in Gibraltar should in no way imply that these men were typically engaged away from enemy action—quite the contrary.

Working in close cooperation with the British Royal Engineers, whose efforts never ceased, the Canadian sappers removed over 140,000 tons of material during their stay at Gibraltar, which ended with their return to England in mid-December 1942. The length of roadways within the Rock is estimated to be equal to that of all of Gibraltar's main exterior road systems, about thirty miles.

Governor Mason-Macfarlane paid special tribute to the RCE Tunnelling Unit in a formal presentation of the Keys to the Fort of Gibraltar, which entitled the men to wear a unique symbol of the Gibraltar Keys as an arm badge on their uniform. This was high praise, the Keys being part of the Gibraltar Coat of Arms and of the historical pageantry celebrated daily at the main gate to the town's old fortification wall. Even during the war, when the gate was never locked, this afternoon ceremony of the Closing of the Gate continued: the Keeper of the Keys (with an escort) approaches the gate, where he is challenged by a guard:

"Halt, who goes there?"

"The Keeper of the Keys," replies the escort party.

"Whose keys?"

"His Sovereign Majesty King George's Keys," replies the escort.

"Approach, Keeper of Keys," says the guard, "and secure the gate."

This type of formality, of course, seems a natural target for disruption by idle troops, and I happened to witness one such ceremony-turned-protest. The object of the protest was the inexhaustible supply of a tinned meat and vegetable stew of dubious vintage, common fare in most messes; rumour held that World War One veterans remembered it well. Military outposts with limited access to refrigeration or other methods of food preservation saw a great deal of tinned bully beef and tinned McConnachie Stew. On this particular Gibraltar afternoon, a couple of soldiers stood on the fort wall walkway, above the gate. While others attended the procession in respectful silence, these fellows watched the ceremony with a more jovial interest, having obviously spent the afternoon fortifying their morale with more than a few noggins of beer.

"Halt, who goes there?" shouted the guard.

"The Keeper of the Keys," replied the escort party.

"Whose keys?" called the guard—and before the escort party could respond, the soldiers leapt at their chance—

"McConna-KEYS!" they bellowed. "The same son-of-a-bitch that covers the world in stew!" Military Police promptly removed the gleeful pair, while the ceremony proceeded amid general chuckles and a barely restrained grin on the face of the officer playing Keeper of the Keys. Today the gates are no longer locked, but the ritual remains.

Other than their presentation with the Keys of the Fort of Gibraltar, I am unaware of any other plaque or symbol of appreciation recording the vital role that the Royal Canadian Engineers played by constructing essential military structures at Gibraltar in the war years of 1941–42. They were not the kind to seek any special acknowledgement. But we who knew the absolute necessity of an operational aircraft runway to the success of the North African invasion (Operation TORCH) can support General Dwight Eisenhower's statement that without that facility the North African operation would not have been possible.

CHAPTER FOUR

DUBIOUS ENCOUNTERS

Given its geographical position, many aircraft flew to Gibraltar and onward to North Africa, Malta, Egypt, the Far East, and other war destinations. The route became much travelled, particularly after the Allied occupation of North Africa in November '42. Prior to that, transit flights had an element of challenge and uncertainty that resulted in all manner of tragedy and adventure. For many crews, these flights were the first phase of entering the atmosphere of live operations, of leaving the shelter of training programs to face new challenges, gaining skill and confidence in the real hazards of war. Thus, these flights are a vital piece of the mosaic that is the history of air war.

In a Hudson aircraft at a cruising speed of 155 knots, the average flying time from RAF Station Portreath—near Land's End in southwest England—to Gibraltar was 7 hours and 15 minutes. Our usual route sent us to a position fifteen miles seaward off the northwest tip of Spain, then southward down the coast to Portugal, around Cape St. Vincent, and east to Gibraltar. An extra 110-gallon fuel tank extended the normal cruising range by 330 nautical miles. Fuel range was not a problem, but other dangers were reason enough for careful flight planning for avoidance of enemy aircraft over the Bay of Biscay and south to Portugal. Enemy aircraft in this area were mostly Ju-88s but sometimes ME 110s (which had shorter range) and occasionally Focke Wulf 200s (which were used for attacking convoys).

German long-range fighters from the Brest area of France operated in Bay of Biscay to intercept our anti-submarine patrols and transient aircraft. These flights of six with Ju-88s and ME 110s were deadly if there was no cloud cover in which to escape. The probability of such an encounter was not great, but our losses were enough to keep us vigilant during that stretch of the flight. On return transient flights from Gibraltar to England, while delivering aircraft for scheduled maintenance or picking up replacements, I met only one aircraft.

We were about a hundred miles south of Cornwall at the first light of dawn, seven thousand feet above six-tenths cloud; breakfast was only an hour away. Suddenly, an aircraft appeared about a half-mile ahead at an angle to cross our track about 1500 feet below and ahead. It was a Henkel 111.

Alert! Alert! Bogey eleven o'clock, half mile—the crew alive in seconds. The six-and-a-half hours of night isolation evaporated in an instant. The procedure in fighting engagements was well rehearsed and automatic in a one-on-one, or if we had a surprise advantage to make an attack. Our practice was to be the aggressor. The pilot's action mostly automatic reflex: auto pilot off—mixture controls auto rich—propellers climb RPM—throttles climb power—seat harness tight. Commence manoeuvre to gain best attack position. Fuel selector to full tank—ring gun sight to aim position—gun button on fire—pilot's sliding window opened an inch. (This last action sucked the cockpit clear of the gun smoke and cordite fumes spewed by the Hudson's inside-mounted guns.) Crew oxygen masks and goggles in place on all crew. Crew reports: Wireless op—*Aerial stored, manning belly gun;*

Turret—*Bogey sighted, turret set*; Navigator—*Mid-gun or cockpit skipper?* (This question, directed to the pilot, determined whether the navigator took up a position to help or to man a mid-cabin window gun, a gun normally used only in defence against a fighter attack.)

We'd closed to about seven hundred yards behind the Henkel when it saw us and immediately dove into cloud. I resumed our heading for RAF Portreath, Cornwall. Soon we were nicely back on course.

"Glad that bugger took off, Skipper," said the navigator with a note of relief. "Could have been a bad doo."

I was surprised by what seemed like an out-of-character fainthearted comment. "What the hell do you mean? No one fired a shot."

"I know, Sir, but with six cases of wine and booze in the spares boxes, it could have been an unfortunate loss."

I should have known—liquor in all forms was cheap and in good supply at Gibraltar,[†] so I now had a smuggling operation on my hands. Time for a quick crew meeting on the intercom.

"What are you nitwits trying to do? Get me demoted or court-martialled? You'd best get your contraband down the flare chute and into the ocean before we make landfall."

The silence on the intercom told me that their morale had suffered a severe blow.

"Please, Skipper," the gunner finally spoke up, "it's not like you think. We checked with some chums in transit control at Portreath. Word is that no questions asked if no money changes hands, strictly presents only."

With some misgivings I swallowed my Presbyterian con-

[†] This was probably a mixture of wine and whiskey; we could buy whiskey at Gibraltar, while wine came in from Spain.

science. "Okay. You had better bloody well be right. If not, you take the rap—I won't even know you."

The following day we delivered the Hudson to RAF Gosport for overhaul, and I travelled north to Scotland for a week's leave. When I arrived at RAF Leuchars in a borrowed Anson, I discovered with my luggage a case of twelve of the best.

TAKING FLAK FROM FORCE H

Throughout the first two months of 1942, our squadron was mostly employed in flying protection patrols for naval and merchant ships and searching for U-boats; in these months, our aircraft managed to maintain experienced crews. But as the year progressed, workloads increased as losses mounted. One harmless encounter, though, was cause for some amused faces in the ops room after I'd arrived back from an area sweep for U-boats ahead of Royal Navy Force H. Comprised of battleships, cruiser, aircraft carriers and destroyers, Force H patrolled the western 500 nautical miles of the Mediterranean to counter Italian naval forces if they came into contact. In a 1941 engagement, the Italians had fared badly and since that time had not been venturesome. When returning to Gibraltar or the Atlantic, the Royal Navy force came into the narrowing of the Mediterranean, where vigilant enemy submariners would patiently wait, undetected. U-boat successes here were stark evidence of their presence; several navy ships, including the *Ark Royal* aircraft carrier, had been lost in the western Mediterranean, where evasive manoeuvres for large ships was difficult.

The other hazard to Force H was air strikes: except for the heavy casualties of men and ships on the Malta convoy (when no alternative was possible), the Royal Navy was cautious about being caught within range of land-based aircraft—German and Italian bombers—without a strong defence of aircraft fighter cover. This lesson had been driven home by the loss of a total force of cruisers and destroyers in the eastern Mediterranean when, evacuating our forces from Crete without any air cover, they were sunk by German Ju-88 aircraft. With the consequences of a skilled air attack clear, the location and movement of Force H was always a carefully held secret.

On this particular occasion, I flew directly towards Force H to make contact before departing for base. Except for actual combat, Force H maintained wireless silence and relayed messages via its escorting aircraft. The procedure required us to approach head-on and, at one mile, fire the coloured recognition Veri cartridge of the day. I flashed a prescribed recognition letter from our Addis signalling lamp as added assurance. I had little faith in the protection this gave us. On two previous occasions, the various identification signals simply alerted some trigger-happy anti-aircraft gunners on the Allied cruiser and destroyers to our presence; they then welcomed us with a barrage of flack (what today is euphemistically termed "friendly fire").

In this instance, too, Force H had not ignored us, and we'd been greeted with a short helping of ack-ack. We circled until things quieted down, then proceeded to signal the flag ship with our lamp. Typically the wireless operator sent the signals, though sometimes I did it myself, sending Morse Code from a hand-held lamp from the front of the cockpit. When signalling, we had to turn in an arc ahead of the ship to set up a line of sight; we'd usually signal the 'flag' ship. Sometimes this required more than one pass. We could send about twenty words a minute and used abbreviated forms—such as "SOS" with the letter U, meaning you are heading into danger ahead. I once alerted destroyers in the North Sea that there were three mines ahead of them; I sent them "U" and they blew up the mines.

Today the signalled message was clear: "Any messages for Gibraltar?" We took their signal-lamp reply and departed. Radio silence was never broken except in emergencies of gravest nature. And I wasn't annoyed at getting fired on; they had a good reason to be safe first and sorry later! In the routine debriefing back at North Front, I mentioned the anti-aircraft ack-ack reception but commented that it was "no problem."

The Admiral who had appeared to get the latest report of Force H was ruffled. "What do you mean, 'no problem'?"

These encounters were never adversarial. He was a very senior officer, and it would be wrong and unintentional to cast him in an unfavourable vein here. The Admiral was a super patriot, a Britannia-Rules-the-Waves and go-down-with-the-ship kind of fellow; however, I am not convinced that he fully understood the use of air power in war, other than as an adjunct of navy or army operations.

I said that the shooting was erratic and that I hadn't felt endangered. He seemed disturbed and—though I'm not sure—took umbrage that I was unscathed.

CHAPTER FIVE

BEATING
THE U-BOATS

Although our Squadron was occasionally given tasks other than shipping protection, our main purpose was to seek and attack enemy submarines (U-boats) in our zone of operations, as these were destroying the maritime lifeline on which Gibraltar and Malta depended. The contest between U-boats and anti-submarine forces was an unrelenting hunt-and-kill struggle on both sides of the conflict, challenging the wit, skill, and courage of all involved.

While concentrating their U-boat forces in the North Atlantic, the German Navy hadn't ignored the Mediterranean as an opportune area to use submarines to blockade Malta and to take a heavy toll on merchant and navy vessels. Within the range of our aircraft (the operational range of Hudsons limited us to 500 nautical miles east or west of Gibraltar), we were able to give some protection to shipping and to contain the U-boat aggression. But beyond our range they operated free from air attack, their only adversaries our Royal Navy destroyers, which escorted supply ship convoys.

Between late 1941 and the spring of 1944, the German *Kreigsmarine* sent 63 U-boats into the Mediterranean. The passage through the Strait of Gibraltar was particularly hazardous where the Royal Navy maintained constant patrols with surface vessels and swordfish aircraft. Upper levels of water current leaving the Strait flows west at a rate that

made it difficult or impossible for a U-boat to traverse the
danger zone while underwater. Their battery capacity for
submerged electrical propulsion was insufficient for them
to traverse the distance without surfacing to recharge the
batteries. However, going through the Strait at night and in
visibility-limiting weather, 40 of the 63 U-boats sent to the
Mediterranean made the passage (10 others were attack-
damaged and returned to their French port; 9 were sunk in
the Strait, and 4 more destroyed in various operations).

The average number of operational U-boats throughout
1941 was about 21, with a further 3 or 4 positioned in the
Atlantic, west of Gibraltar. Within the Mediterranean, 12
submarines covered an area of about a hundred nautical miles
from Alboran Island, which rises midway between Spain
and North Africa, 90 miles offshore. This U-boat blockade
required extreme vigilance by Allied ships, who became prey
in this confined water. Even when all our protective measures
were in use, daring U-boat commanders pressed home torpedo attacks, with hard results. On November 14, 1941, the *Ark
Royal* Force H aircraft carrier was sunk while on a protected
approach to Gibraltar. The loss of such capital ships—while
damaging the Royal Navy's Force H strength—fuelled the
determination for retribution and the urgency to increase
anti-U-boat aircraft operating from Gibraltar.

A DEADLY GAME OF HIDE-AND-SEEK

Up until the arrival of two more Hudson squadrons, the
number of available aircraft to find and attack enemy submarines was simply inadequate to provide the level of protection
needed. And while we developed our hunting and attacking
skills to counter the U-boats, they had also improved their
technology and tactical methods to avoid detection and to

FIGURE 7

233 Squadron flew Hudsons effectively in
U-boat search and destroy missions.

defend against aircraft. They could detect our radar and, if employed to fight on the surface, their anti-aircraft guns could be lethal.

To detect U-boats from the air, we used both radar and constant eyeball scanning of the sea surface, looking for the smallest persistent white feather of a periscope which radar would not detect. If a blip came on the radar scope, it was prudent to immediately note the distance and turn off the radar to eliminate the possibility of alerting the target's radar pulse detector. From there on, we scanned for the earliest visual contact, aiming for an unseen approach and attack.

High-power binoculars were of no assistance in an initial sighting; they were cumbersome, restricted in view span, and distracting in practical use. But a plain visual search could be greatly improved by a practised technique of near and far sector sweeping of a forward arc of about 45° either side of dead-ahead, then a glance at instruments in the cockpit, and some relief eye rest by rapidly blinking and squeezing the eyelids to retain moisture, as altering your vision range can improve sighting at all distances.

Experience had taught us that when U-boats were sighted, their look-out would almost certainly see the aircraft and be able to crash-dive before the aircraft could attack on the surface. Some of our squadron's losses came from pressing home an attack on a surfaced U-boat recharging its batteries; while vulnerable, it prepared its anti-aircraft guns for a surfaced fight. In this kind of attack encounter, victory often meant survival, and on several occasions the duel ended with both parties being killed.

In some respects, submarine and aircraft shared certain tactical advantages; both operated alone and were dependent on their own knowledge and skills, their commitment and courage often leading to their unobserved death. However, twice in the Mediterranean a U-boat commander, after being damaged and unable to submerge, surrendered to save his crew. In doing so, he disobeyed Hitler's "No surrender" orders, with fatal consequences. (An account of one such incident is given later in this chapter.)

Gaining visual contact with the submarine before it detected us was an obvious advantage, but in normal conditions our advantage was marginal. In daylight hours, the U-boats tended to travel partially submerged, with only the conning tower showing, and the whole vessel could be underwater in a little over a minute. To make a killing attack, we had to release the depth charges over the U-boat before it could dive below the lethal range of the explosives, which were set to detonate at 50 feet below the surface and to rupture or disable a hull 30 to 50 feet from the charge. It was a stealth-and-pounce game of cat and mouse, only these "mice" were themselves deadly predators.

Experienced aircraft pilots were acutely aware of all the conditions that could tilt the odds in their favour: the position of the sun and clouds, the state of the sea and the wind, wave spray, the course of the submarine, as well as general weather conditions such as rain or haze. With visibility five miles or more, the best patrol altitude for a Hudson aircraft was about 5,000 feet; this optimum height was determined by the typical detectible distance of the aircraft. If the cloud bottoms were below 5,000 feet, our usual practice was to fly just below the clouds. Altitude, aircraft profile, and low reflectivity of the paint colour established the angle above the horizon where we were least visible. On occasion—if out of sun, or if downwind, or in rough sea conditions where waves and spray would hamper the submarine's look-out and air-defence guns—the aircraft would quickly change course, hoping to remain unseen and to reposition itself for a best-direction attack.

It is, of course, not possible to include an account of all incidents of aircraft and U-boat encounters, many of which have two sides to stories not known until the war ended. In some combat incidents, the outcome was unknown at the time of happening but later determined by information from various sources, validated by reports and documents from post-war enemy files; in other cases, a clearer sense of what had taken place came from discovery of identifiable aircraft and wreckage in waters where our aircraft disappeared, and from the eyewitness accounts of survivors and neutral observers. In the years after the war, Spanish fishing boats encountered debris in their nets that explained the loss of two of our crews, one shot down on a U-boat attack, the other showing evidence of an encounter with a German Henkel 111 also found in the area. It seems most probable that they destroyed each other.

Owing to the solitary nature of our missions, most of our losses remained unsolved.

MAY DAY, 1942

On the first day of May, Sergeant Brent attacked a submarine at a position about 350 nautical miles east of Gibraltar (37° N—01.00W) The U-boat was crippled in the attack and, after resurfacing, its crew appeared on deck waving a white flag of surrender. The submarine appeared badly damaged and incapable of submerging or manoeuvring. Sergeant Brent circled for more than twenty minutes, then returned to Gibraltar on completion of his patrol. At the Operations

Room debriefing, the Air Officer Commanding Gibraltar congratulated the sergeant on a well-executed attack. But the Rear Admiral, also attending the debriefing, wasn't so congratulatory. "Sergeant, why didn't you machine-gun those on deck?"

This Rear Admiral was frequently present at pre-flight briefings and returning-crews debriefings. His particular interest concerned our aircraft's contact and escort duties with the Navy Force H, and his show-them-no-mercy policy was at times more than vehement.

Brent simply looked at me, his squadron commander, for a response.

"My squadron," I said in a matter-of-fact tone to the Admiral, "does not shoot prisoners."

The Air Officer Commanding (AOC), Air Commodore Simpson, intervened. "It's quite possible that the U-boat is still afloat, and we can't get a surface vessel to that location in less than ten hours. How soon can you get airborne to search for the submarine and sink it if necessary?"

I told him I could be off the ground in thirty minutes with my standby crew. When I reached the dispersal fifteen minutes later, Sergeant Warren had his crew settled in the Hudson AM 575. The navigator, Sergeant Frew, was given a fresh chart, with the area of search marked by operation-room staff (in the coordination of air and sea operations, a combined staff directed and monitored operations).

Our flight, mostly at night, relied on Air to Surface Vessel radar (ASV) to detect anything on the surface. I decided to have Sergeant Warren fly within a hundred miles of the U-boat location, at which point I'd take control for the rest of the sortie. Warren's crew were recent arrivals on the squadron, and this was their first standby duty. The intention was to keep them fully committed to the flight schedule, but this operation was special, and my experience on the Hudson aircraft and in attack situation would be useful.

A routine flight at 5,000 feet to the area of probability was uneventful. At that height, we had a good ASV scan of more than fifteen miles on small targets. Our planned search was to start at the last known position on the submarine with a creeping line ahead on a visual distance of eight (v8). We'd advance eastward two V (sixteen miles) one each forty-mile parallel leg, starting at the coast. The approach to the starting point was from ten miles out and followed the coast until opposite the attack location.

We assumed two things: (1) that if the U-boat could move either under reduced power or towed by another vessel, it would not exceed five knots; and (2) that the U-boat was incapable of submerging and would proceed to the nearest safe haven—not northward to open sea but probably to the coast, toward Algiers. (The direction westward toward Oran had been thoroughly checked when outbound.)

After completing these forty-mile search lines, there was nothing to investigate in the area we'd covered. I was convinced we hadn't missed any object that could be our target; however, to be sure of every reasonable possibility, I decided to do two more sweep lines of twenty miles. When turning at the end of the first additional sweep, the navigator came to the intercom with a note of concern.

"Skipper, the wind has increased ten to fifteen knots and now three fifteen degrees."

This meant headwinds on the way back and reduced ground speed, adding forty-five minutes to the return flight. I realized that I'd used all our reserve fuel in prolonging the search, and I immediately turned for a direct course to Gibraltar.

We'd been in the air for four hours and fifteen minutes, and a quick calculation showed at least another four-fifteen to North Front. By reducing the engine RPM to 1650, and by leaning the fuel-air mixture to the limit, we could remain airborne for a total of eight hours and forty-five minutes—meaning we were quite possibly in for a night ditching east of Gibraltar. Another option was to lighten our load by releasing the depth charges, though this would give no more than another five minutes of flying time. If ditching became inevitable, the load of depth charges would have to be jettisoned beforehand. It occurred to me that, in an overzealous attempt to complete Sergeant Brent's effort to destroy the U-boat, I'd stretched the bounds of good judgement and now could lose an airplane without any achievement.

Gibraltar was dead ahead twelve miles, with the fuel gauge reaching for empty. Throttling back a straight-in approach and landing, we touched down at eight hours and thirty-one minutes with ten minutes of fuel remaining, accompanied by smiles from crew positions in the dim light.

Contrary to our assumptions, the U-boat had limped northeast, in the least likely direction. The U-boat (later identified as 573) hadn't been found because—though heavily damaged and incapable of diving—it was able to beach itself on the coast of Spain. A few days after its attack, British diplomats were made aware that German U-boat 4-573 had limped, seriously damaged, into the Spanish port of Cartagena; Sergeant Brent's attack had indeed destroyed the U-boat, and it was not repairable in the time allowed by non-belligerent countries for servicing wartime vessels. However, Spain had made an unusual concession in this case, which of course invoked heated protest from the British. Spain then withdrew its concession for the extended repair. As the U-boat would remain interned for the duration of the war,

Germany removed its torpedoes and sold the submarine to Spain for a token price; Spain then completed the necessary repair and used the submarine in its own navy.

The crew and the commander of U-573, Kpt/Lt Heinrick Heinsohn, returned to Germany. In *Kriegsmarine* documents, the crew report of the attack and of subsequent events gives a fabricated story that must have involved a vow of secrecy by those involved. There is no mention of their surrender; instead, they describe fighting off the attacking aircraft and nursing the crippled boat to the Spanish harbour. The date of the attack is also falsified as April 29, rather than May 1. The reasons for that deceit remains unknown; however, their motive for lying about their surrender is well understood, as Hitler issued orders that required them to fight to the death if unable to submerge.

For Kpt/Lt Heinsohn, the reprieve was short. Three months later, the U-boat he was commanding was discovered by RAF aircraft and sunk in the North Atlantic. As for Sergeant Brent, his contribution to our cause was not given any special award; he and his crew were lost in action two months later.

U-BOAT PUZZLE

By June 1942, the numbers and capability of 233 Squadron significantly deterred the U-boats' ability to operate. In 1941 the enemy had lost 3 U-boats attempting passages through the Gibraltar Strait, with 4 more sunk in the Mediterranean; they still had 21 operational, but the tide of battle was slowly turning in our favour. By the end of 1942, the Germans sent a total of 40 U-boats into the Mediterranean, but the number available to function remained at 21. For this twelve-month period, the Germans saw 15 of their submarines sunk and a number damaged from both aircraft and surface vessel attacks. During this same period, the Germans sent in 18 U-boats to augment their numbers; 16 of these managed to pass through the Strait, while 2 turned back. Their unusually high rate of success in crossing that very dangerous stretch of water puzzled our vigilant U-boat hunters.

Only after the war was it discovered that U-boat crews knew that lower flow levels of the Strait could be favourable to an east-bound submarine. An anomaly of this wartime advantage for the U-boats was that at war's end none had ever left the Mediterranean; all had ended either destroyed or scuttled.

And so, while the decisive battle against U-boats was the vital priority now known as "the Battle of the Atlantic," a critical struggle was taking place on a smaller scale in the Mediterranean, with equal fervour and with similar results. In the Atlantic, the sinking of forty-one U-boats during May 1943 saw air attacks responsible for more than half of all submarines destroyed; in the Mediterranean, our success with air attacks on U-boats grew with our increasing air dominance in both numbers and in technique of detection and weapon delivery.

In all this, both sides paid the price of human lives, survivors growing callouses of tolerance for the brutality of war. We couldn't afford the weight of compassion while delivering death to a crew of forty in a U-boat's crowded iron tomb; nor did the U-boat crew view the destruction of ships and aircraft as anything other than pragmatic victory to be applauded.

These German U-boats had the ability to cripple Allied shipping in the western Mediterranean and to deplete the fighting strength of the Allies in North East Africa. This affliction was coupled with enemy air forces in the mid and eastern areas extending from Sicily to Crete, also effective in attacking ships. Resolving the dilemma of our own offensive capability in the Mediterranean was dependent on the success of operation TORCH.

CHAPTER SIX

CONVOYS & AIRCRAFT

If there was ever any doubt about the absolute necessity of having air power to survive and succeed in military conflicts, the experiences of air and sea warfare in the Mediterranean of 1941–42 leave no lack of proof. And flying protection for ships en route to Malta were, for me, the most challenging of our commitments. We protected to the limit of our range, yet always with a sense of inadequacy because we knew that when we left them, they headed into the certainty of attacks and heavy losses. Our aircraft were able to fly patrols and ship protection out to a distance of about five hundred and fifty nautical miles, only halfway to Malta. The rest of the route was by far the most hazardous, as much of the remaining distance was within range of the German and Italian aircraft based in Sicily and Tunisia. The more confined areas near Malta saw grim sea battles and shipping losses to U-boats, to aircraft attack, and to mines. One look at a map of the Mediterranean Sea makes the hazard for convoys and their escorts readily apparent. Tennyson's "Charge of the Light Brigade" had its counterpart in these nautical jaws of hell. But these convoys *had* to try to reach Malta.

Malta, of course, was the strategic keystone to the outcome of the Mediterranean conflict. If it were to continue to fight off invasion, then sacrifices of ships and lives had to be made in order to bring in essential supplies. The struggle for survival of the vital Malta base was one of great fortitude, sacrifice, and heroism and changed the course of World War Two; the full story of its defence has been well documented. The Spitfire fighters and other defence armaments arriving in Malta in June of 1942 helped inflict an increasingly heavy toll on the enemy, making possible the turning of the fortunes of war in our favour. In this, the Royal Navy lived up to its tradition for daring and toughness; both ships and men gave no quarter and sought none.

As for my own role, being part of the Western Mediterranean and Atlantic approaches on daily operations gave me a first-hand acquaintance with the grim reality of ships lost to enemy attacks. It is difficult to imagine anything with more impact to affirm the importance of our mission than the sight of burning and sinking vessels, seamen drowning, while from air we could do nothing but try to destroy the underwater killers and direct the surface vessels to recover as many crew as possible.

When picking up survivors, the rescuers became sitting targets themselves, and convoy escort ships were often required to delay or leave rescue activities and remain on station to protect the remaining convoy, no matter what the circumstances. Such orders seemed brutally pragmatic or heartless, a wrenching moral dilemma, the reality of war. Still, many of the torpedoed or bombed ships' crews did manage to get rescued from the water and returned to Gibraltar, brave merchant mariners, unheralded and unsung. We frequently saw them in the street in their new issue of clothing, having their few days ashore while awaiting another sea-duty assignment.

Convoy losses have been well documented; less so—and more vivid—are memories of two convoys of about fourteen ships each, described below, which tried to take desperately needed supplies to Malta. Fewer than five ships survived.

THE *Wasp* AND THE *Eagle*

Churchill and his military strategists were acutely aware of the urgency to deliver Spitfires to Malta. They also knew that the only way to do this was by using naval aircraft carriers to transport the Spitfires within flying range of the Islands, launching from the carrier within five hundred miles. From there, with additional fuel in a slipper tank attached by releasable latches to the belly of the aircraft, the Spitfires could over-fly the crucial ship danger zone to Malta, with a forty-minute reserve for emergency delay or combat.

The crux of the Spitfire delivery problem was the critical shortage of aircraft carriers. With the loss of the *Audicity* and *Ark Royal*, and with the seriously damaged *Indomitable* and *Illustrious*, the only available carrier for Spitfire delivery was the old, 22,000-ton *Eagle*, whose maximum capacity was about twenty-five aircraft. Without a more substantial replenishment for the Malta squadrons, the retention of the Islands was in jeopardy. As a stop-gap measure, Churchill asked President Roosevelt for the emergency use of an American carrier. The United States Navy (USN) had a pressing need for all of their carriers for the Pacific War, but the President approved a special concession to have the USN *Wasp* make two trips for Spitfires to Malta. This commitment was extremely important as the *Wasp* (a small, modern ship of 14,700 tons) could take about forty-five aircraft on her 100-foot-wide by 720-foot-long deck. On April 13, 1942, she left Glasgow, Scotland, for the Mediterranean loaded with forty-seven Spitfires and their pilots. The importance of her mission was recognized by the strong escort of cruisers *Rowan*, *Charybdis*, *Cairo*, and destroyers.

The aircraft pilots on this venture came from all over the Commonwealth and the British Isles; they had no experience of flying from aircraft carriers and knew little of where, how, and when until the ship was well underway. (I knew several who were in this Shanghaied lot of aviators, including one from my own hometown; many were Canadians who later became known for their combat exploits in Malta and elsewhere in the Mediterranean theatre.)

Early on the morning of April 19, the *Wasp*, commanded by Captain J.W. Reeves Jr. of the United States Navy cleared the Strait of Gibraltar. My first escort of the Spitfire delivery carriers took place on April 20 when, on a rotation schedule with other escorts from our squadron, I picked up the flotilla shortly after she had completed the dispatch of her forty-seven aircraft cargo. Our task on these escort sorties was to sweep for U-boats several miles ahead of the ships by flying a progression of parallel tracks horizontal to the ship's direction. On this delivery, one Spitfire failed to reach Malta, but the fleet returned to Gibraltar without any other casualties or mishap.

A few weeks later, on May 8, we made another delivery attempt. This time the *Wasp* was loaded up with forty-five Spitfires, accompanied by the *Eagle* with nineteen. Both carriers proceeded eastward under the same escort. Once again, their mission was a success, though there was an unexplained loss of three Spitfires.

One unusual Spitfire incident raised the question of auxiliary fuel-supply failure, a failure that would leave the aircraft with insufficient range to make Malta. All the Spitfires on that delivery had been shipped in wooden crates to Gibraltar where they were reassembled with wings and flown prior to being loaded onto the carriers. Although this did not preclude the possibility of some future malfunction, nothing in the preparation for the flights from ships to Malta was untested—yet failures do occur.

Two brother pilots from British Columbia, Robert and Jerrold Smith, formed part of the *Wasp* contingent. At a later date, Robert related the following description of the incident. Shortly after becoming airborne from the *Wasp*, Flying Officer Jerrold Smith turned on the auxiliary slipper tank, and immediately the merlin engine stopped, due to fuel starvation. By returning to the regular tanks, the motor resumed power, but without the slipper fuel, he couldn't reach Malta. After several attempts to solve the problem, Smith determined that the malfunction couldn't be fixed, and he continued to fly around the ship until all the other Spitfires had left.

Smith was not only a good pilot but also one with much self-confidence, and he decided that he could land back on the carrier if they'd let him try. But he'd have to indicate his problem and his intentions without any radio communication, as the order to maintain "radio silence" with ships was a security that could not be violated. His first task was to jettison the slipper tank along with its fuel in full view of the ship; he did this with a low pass alongside. He then had to seek some sign of approval for his attempt to land back on board. The ship would have realized his problem in seeing the tank dropped; his next slow fly-by alongside the ship took place with wheels down and wing wagging. Smith left the undercarriage wheels down as he circled; in response, the ship turned about 20 degrees to starboard, directly into the 15-knot winds, and flashed a green light on the signal lamp. The *Wasp* skipper, Captain Reeves, was a man of gallant nature; if this bold kid pilot was willing to try landing an airplane without arrester-gear, he'd give him the chance.

With the *Wasp* doing 30 knots and with a wind of 15 knots, the total of 45 knots and the Spitfire's final approach speed of 70 knots, there would be a 25-knot deck speed to arrest the aircraft. And Jerrold Smith did it! The ship's captain and crew were delighted with this young Canadian who didn't understand that land-based aircraft were not supposed to be flown onto carriers by unqualified pilots.

Meanwhile at Malta and Gibraltar, Jerrold Smith was posted as missing; the same radio-silence edict that guarded the position of the ship also prevented transmission of Smith's location on the *Wasp*, where he was dubbed an honorary naval aviator. When within range, he took off for Gibraltar, there to be met with some astonishment. Fortunately, he had a letter with him from Capt. Reeves, verifying the circumstances. I regret to say that this able pilot, who went to Malta on the *Eagle*'s last delivery, was later killed in action.

After her second Spitfire delivery of 45 aircraft on May 9, accompanied by the *Eagle* with nineteen aircraft, the *Wasp* departed for the war in the Pacific, where three months later she was sunk by Japanese torpedoes. And on August 11, the old aircraft carrier *Eagle*, which had made six deliveries of Spitfires, was hit by at least two torpedoes on a return run and went down. I recall seeing her listing at a steep angle and slowly submerging, a Swordfish aircraft on her titled deck, escort destroyers circling to find her killer. This particular loss cut me: a brave and fatally wounded old warrior in her death throes, while her smaller protectors hovered, futile, and could not save her. An indelible image.

Thus ended the services of *Wasp* 15 September 1942 and *Eagle* 11 August 1942, two carriers that performed their duty brave and undaunted. The *Wasp* took a total of 94 aircraft for Malta, while the old *Eagle,* in May and June of '42, had delivered 91. We who escorted these gallants will remember them.

JULY 1942: FROM GIBRALTAR TO MALTA

Throughout the first two months of 1942, our squadron was mostly employed in flying protection patrols for naval and merchant ships and searching for U-boats; in these months our aircraft losses managed to maintain experienced crews. But as the year progressed, workloads increased as losses mounted. By the beginning of July, the runway continued to lengthen, and the infrastructure for receiving and accommodating aircraft grew to keep pace with an increasing flow of transients through North Front. The role of our Gibraltar airfield as the essential staging point for Malta-bound aircraft added significant strength to Malta's ability to strike and destroy enemy ships that supplied their African forces.

While the Spitfires defending Malta had to be delivered halfway from Gibraltar by aircraft carriers, longer-range aircraft could now be delivered with little or no hindrance: Wellingtons, Beaufighters, and Blenems could fly directly to Malta after refuelling at Gibraltar. These aircraft, along with the Royal Navy's three submarines operating from Malta, were so effective in attacks on Axis shipping that both German and Italian senior commanders believed that their armies in North Africa could not be sustained while Malta remained unconquered. There is no doubt, then, that the combined use of air power to defend Malta and to cripple the enemy was strategic to the outcome of the war in the Mediterranean and in Africa.

A fortuitous decision saw Air Vice Marshall Keith Parks take command of this air battle in early July. He was probably the most tested tactical and strategic air commander in confronting vastly superior numbers in a do-or-die struggle. Parks, a New Zealander, never lost confidence or the common touch. During the Battle of Britain he was Air Commander of the Eleven Group aircraft that bore the brunt of the fighting in the late summer of 1940, which staved off the invasion of England. He was one of the very few senior air officers who flew his own Spitfire. And there is a widely held feeling that acknowledgement of this man's achievement and leadership has been most modest.

A DIM VIEW

An operational tour of duty for our squadron was usually limited to 450 hours. However, at times the intensity of consecutive flying days could be over-tiring, and extra time off, or a few days away on scheduled aircraft maintenance in the United Kingdom, gave a badly needed break. Another option was to post a person nearing his tour limit as "tour expired"; if the squadron doctor thought this latter arrangement advisable, he'd counsel the commanding officer. The fact is that individuals handle stress at different levels, and if the functioning of a crew member had obviously deteriorated, a transfer of duty was advised. There were very few instances of early termination of an operational tour, but with too many consecutive flight days, stress levels became a concern.

In general, all crews were scheduled for the same level of sorties, but on occasion some aspect of a sortie meant detailing a special crew. In July of 1942, the load of squadron tasks was demanding for all crews; I flew on twenty days that month, including six-hour patrols on July 13 and 14, then a one-hour test flight on July 15. The next day, I delivered Beaufighter T4666 to Malta, a five-hour flight arriving there at dark—during an air raid.

On crossing Tunis, dusk falling, flying at ten thousand

FIGURE 8

*233 Squadron had two Beaufighter long range escort fighters for
use in convoy protection against Folkwolf 200 and JU88s.*

feet, I spotted a Feisler Storch, a small communication airplane, crossing below me at about five thousand feet. I thought—should I go down and blow him to bits? One short burst with the Beau's four 20-mil cannons and six 303 machine guns would take only two or three minutes. Second thought—what the hell, he won't win the war, and we need this Beaufighter and its ammunition in Malta.

It was after dark when I arrived at the Valletta airfield. With German-Italian aircraft en route from Sicily to make their daily bombing of the Islands, my radio clearance was to land "without delay." The controller made it sound like routine procedure, which I suppose it was, after months of these constant attacks.

I crossed the active runway at about 800 feet in a left descending turn for final approach. My impression was that the runway lights were rather dim— they'd be invisible, I thought, from above seven or eight thousand feet, and I figured this was probably a protective measure. But landing suddenly became a concern: when I completed the final approach, I couldn't see the runway lights until I was too close to make a low-level "line-up" correction of several hundred feet. There was nothing for it but to put on power and go around for another approach.

Not only was I frustrated and embarrassed at having the runway kept open for me when an attack was imminent, but I prided myself as a very competent night and instrument pilot; in fact, instructing this very type of flying and been my prime duty at the Operational Training Unit. On my second approach, I tightened the turn and landed without trouble. At the end of the landing run, an airman with shielded electric flashlights signalled me into a revetment dispersal (a shelter protecting aircraft from strafing by enemy aircraft, in this case formed of banked earth on three sides). It was a warm night, and I was sweating; in reaching to mop my brow, I encountered ... my dark glasses, which I'd left on even after nightfall.

Dim runway lights, indeed. Someone needed advice at the next mirror.

THE MALTA COMMITMENT

My stay was a brief four or five hours, during which I debriefed and had a bully beef sandwich in the underground control bunker. When I'd left Gibraltar to deliver the Beau to Malta, it was with the strict understanding that I couldn't be spared from our squadron for more than forty-eight hours, and an arrangement was made for me, along with crew Sergeant Moore, to take the 24 Squadron Hudson AE581 back to Gibraltar that evening. This unarmed weekly return flight from the UK through the danger zone where enemy fighters could be encountered was always made at night. On this trip, we had eight passengers whose priority for the limited seating was for various urgencies. One was a very pregnant woman who endured the seven-and-a-half hour flight without being offered the relief station at the back of the cabin—damn thoughtless males!

While waiting for a late departure hour from Malta, I met an officer from my pilot training days at RAF Hullavington; he was now commanding the Photo Reconnaissance Unit (PRU) at Malta. With special long-range Spitfires, the PRU photographed enemy formations. Squadron Leader Worthington was a decorated protocol-breaching character whose exploits were notorious. The Malta Spitfire pilots and the air crews of shipping attack aircraft were a mixed legion of Brits, Canadians, Australians, New Zealanders, and Americans—with Canadians comprising a full third of the total. Among the many who flew in the historic defence of Malta were the names of Canadian pilots whose distinguished records are well known; one young pilot officer serving under Worthington in PRU was Bill Carr, who survived to become Lieutenant General in the post war RCAF. Other pilots—such as Stan Turner, who fought in France, the Battle of Britain, Malta, and North Africa—were strong leaders. Buck McNair, Buzz Buerling, and a host of others all played a major part defending the skies of these small islands.

Of the 120 fighter pilots killed, 31 were from Canada, along with 13 Aussies, 11 New Zealanders, 8 Americans and 64 British. A further 35 Beaufighter air crew were lost on shipping attacks and 20 Fleet Air Arm pilots on convoy protection. In the annals of war these numbers seem small, but in terms of heroic proportion in sacrifice and achievement, they are of historic significance. My short visit to Malta left me with a clear feeling of the spirit that imbued all that went on in that beleaguered outpost. Their focus was clear: repel the enemy. Everything was organized to make full use of their limited resources. There was no excess of any commodity, and in their view the way ahead led only to victory.

Back at Gibraltar, the flying tempo continued. Having arrived on the morning of July 17, I had the rest of the day off but flew six-hour patrols on July 18, 19, and 21. In an eight-day period in July, I flew airplanes for 44 hours. But somehow the close look at the Malta commitment made it all worthwhile.

A HIGH PRICE

It is difficult to imagine anything more heroic than the sacrifice made in the fight to get the five supply ships of convoy "Harpoon" into Malta harbour. Out of the fourteen that formed the convoy, seven were sunk and two of the five that managed to get through the continuous assault by enemy ships, U-boats, and aircraft had to be towed into Vanenitia [sic] harbour. The Royal Navy loss was equally horrendous; the cruisers *Manchester* and *Cairo* were lost, with two others damaged. More than 350 people of all ranks were killed and many others wounded.

At times, a convoy's specific needs were of such emergency priority that Royal Navy submarines based at Malta were used for the delivery. On one such urgent run, I escorted the light Cruise Mine layer *Welshman* in full speed at over 40 knots. She was fast enough to make the most dangerous part of the trip in and out during darkness. This extraordinary ship unfortunately fell prey to a torpedo attack while on a run between Malta and Alexandria on February 1, 1943. Because of the need to keep information secure, the extent of the losses was not made public at the time. Only after the war was the veil of security lifted, revealing the true cost in lost convoys of merchant vessels for the first seven months of 1942, as well as the extent of disaster and the human lives lost in Allied efforts to preserve Malta.

Between February and September 1942, thirty merchant ships were in Malta convoys. Ten were sunk en route; ten turned back damaged; ten reached Malta. Of those final ten, three were sunk after arrival, and seven—only seven of the original thirty—survived with cargo intact. And the loss of naval vessels, as already noted for one convoy, was of historic magnitude. In fact, in the miracle of the cross-channel Dunkirk rescue-evacuation of British troops in 1940, naval ship losses were modest when compared to the Mediterranean sea war of 1941 – 42 and were without capital vessels, carriers, battleships, or cruiser casualties. We hear more of the engagements exposed to the public, the victories and defeats that stirred the hearts of a nation at war. On the sea there were the sinkings of the *Hood*, the *Graf Spree*, and the *Bismarck*. The outcome of land battles between British Army forces and the German Africa Corps was daily news in most homes; the bombing siege of Malta was also of grave national concern. But in the turmoil of worldwide conflicts, fierce struggles of critical consequence can be locked in unseen and little-heard-of deadly conflicts. It's not that political and military leaders didn't understand the vital nature of the Mediterranean war, but its volatile and violent encounters with the enemy was not easy to portray in a favourable light, considering the losses incurred.

Nor did the enemy go unscathed. In their attack on the massive convoy (Operation 'Pedestal', from Gibraltar-Malta), which began August 11 and continued into the night of August 13, they lost forty aircraft, a U-boat, and a number of smaller vessels. When within range of Malta, the Spitfires took their share of the attacking bombers in significant numbers. The assessment of the German command, as made known in post-war documents, was that neither side could claim total victory. And the bastion of Malta held.

CHAPTER SEVEN

TARGET: GIBRALTAR

The possibility of causing major destruction in the confined and high density area of the North Front airfield must have been an enticing prospect for air attack. But the very significant targets at both the harbour-dockyard area and the North Front airfield sustained surprisingly little damage in the few air raids made by the Vichy French Navy air fleet aircraft late in 1940 and again in '41 and '42. Yet there can be no doubt that Germans were aware of Gibraltar's increasing air activity and the large number of aircraft and stockpile of materials being assembled here. So why did the *Luftwaffe* not attempt heavy bombing raids?

Perhaps the answer lay in the natural obstacles and defences of Gibraltar: it was indeed a difficult place to bomb. And the flight distance from airfields in France is about 650 nautical miles on a route via the Mediterranean and around the eastern and southern coast of Spain—the flight to Gibraltar and back extended the limits of the Henkel 111 or Ju-88 aircraft that were the mainstays of the German bomber force. An alternate route over Spain would violate that country's neutrality and cause unwanted repercussions in the delicate political balance. Even after arriving at Gibraltar, Spain's neutrality presented another restrictive factor: any bombing run approach on the airfield was limited to a precise, narrow, 2,000-foot-wide strip with Spain on the north and Gib's towering, vertical rock face on the south. These physical features meant that all approaches had to be east-west (or west-east) and all turns made to the south of that line.

Finally, the anti-aircraft gun defences of Gibraltar were formidable, and the predictable area of attack only added to their effectiveness. Harbour area defences were equally deterring—the land based guns had an unrestricted field of fire, and the regular presence of armed naval ships multiplied the anti-aircraft fire power. All in all, Gibraltar was a difficult and dangerous place to attack. And yet it presented one of the most vital and concentrated targets of the war. I know of no post-war explanation for Germany's neglect of this obvious target.

VICHY NAVY AIR BOMBINGS

The Vichy French air squadrons from North Africa airfields near Oran and Port Lyautey attempted revenge air strikes against Gibraltar in late 1940, and again on July 5 and September 24 of '41. These attacks were retaliation for British destruction of French warships berthed in Oran's harbour. (The British had taken this action to prevent any possibility of the ships being added to German sea forces.) When Vichy France didn't store their naval vessels in non-combatant nation anchorages, they became casualties of the British pre-emptive strike. Many international observers of military history believe that the Oran attack touched a raw nerve of centuries-old adversarial conflict and national pride. And what at first may have been mere resentment of the armed power that had crushed Vichy France swiftly grew into a festering animosity. For the French, it became a point of honour to attack Gibraltar.

Obviously, any attack could only be done with aircraft. In the end, the Gibraltar raids did little damage, while three of the attacking aircraft were shot down. And it must be said that not all Vichy French were anti-British; in fact, after the Allied occupation of North Africa, discussion with some junior ranks of Vichy French squadrons confirmed that a considerable percentage of them had little motivation to attack Gibraltar and welcomed the decision to cease such attempts. However, a degree of bitterness with our previous ally was fast becoming hatred, particularly when several vindictive and pointless incidents resulted in the loss of our aircraft, shot down in transit west of Morocco's territorial waters.

The French Navy fighters responsible for these attacks were from Port Lyautey and Agadir squadrons. Two of our crew members had miraculously survived separate crashes into the sea and gave accounts of attacks made in a despicable and cowardly manner. One surviving gunner described intercepting French fighters flying alongside our aircraft with no indication of aggressive intent. Because they were in international space, and the approach and behaviour of the Vichy aircraft was not threatening, our gunners had been instructed by their pilots to "hold fire." Suddenly, in the midst of its ostentatious departure, one of the three fighters passed behind and opened fire from less than fifty yards.

The aircraft made a semi-controlled crash into the sea; the pilot had been wounded, and only the turret gunner survived. He was able to inflate his dinghy life-raft and by pure chance was picked up by a friendly ship that happened to pass within sight of him in daylight hours. The name of the Vichy pilot who committed this act became known to us after our forces occupied Morocco in operation TORCH. At that time, I tried to get permission to take a couple of Beaufighters and make a dawn visit on Port Lyautey with rockets and cannon. My commanding officer was sympathetic to our anger but counselled that a day of reckoning would soon be at hand and that my wrath could wait.

FIRE IN THE MINE FIELD!

1942 saw only two Vichy Navy air-raid bombings on Gibraltar—both at night and directed at the North Front airfield. These were "derring-do" affairs, demonstrating against the British, who had sunk ships in Oran. The first bombing seemed to be a token effort by two or three aircraft dropping small, anti-personnel, shrapnel-type bombs along with some incendiaries. In October we experienced a second attack, this time more serious in the number of aircraft and types of bombs used.

The escalating build-up of aircraft and materials for the North African invasion had created a concentrated stockpile of great importance—all very visible from the Spanish harbour. And because of the limited space, our own squadron's aircraft were also parked close together: all fifteen occupied an area between the eight-foot-high cemetery wall and a squadron office hut sitting a short distance from the Gibraltar-to-Spain road. Tails of the aircraft came within a few paces of a land mine field extending towards Gibraltar. This mined area was covered in coils of barbed wire with a heavy growth of bamboo-like cane growing through it; tinder dry and twice as tall as an average man. This anti-invasion obstruction gave some security to our parking compound but was not the neighbourhood of choice for our armed, bomb-loaded aircraft. Still, there were no perfect solutions to location problems, and we accepted without question (or alternative) this typical balancing of risk against expediency, which is the common flavour of war.

The raid took place shortly after dark on a clear October

night, sirens sounding only minutes before the first bombs fell. Gibraltar's geography, a peninsula without any extending land mass, made difficult any early warning of approaching hostile aircraft. The proximity of non-hostile Spanish aircraft flying in the international area surrounding Gibraltar added to this dilemma and negated the effectiveness of any electronic detection system. Air-raid shelters were few and crude in the North Front area, most only elongated holes dug in the sand of the isthmus and covered with wood and a top layer of soil. In the town, shelter for thousands could be found in the caves and tunnel excavations, but here at the airfield such shelter was not a priority; perhaps due to the rare occurrence of raids. Still, the anti-aircraft guns and searchlights were alert and regularly practised shooting against aircraft-towed rogue targets. (On several occasions, I flew searchlight training exercises for the defence crews.)

When this raid started, I was in the officer mess hut reading a magazine, focussed on gentle care of a digestive system just in the early stage of conquering a second encounter with the dreaded intestinal scours. I'd barely made it out of the building when a stick of small bombs, probably fifty kilos, landed to the east of the operations building.

In the next few minutes more were dropped. They seemed to be a mixture of incendiaries and, judging by the sound, some larger types of a hundred kilos or more. Most were falling in the western part of the airfield, filling the air with dust. Fires started, and my only thought was that our own aircraft—with full fuel and depth charges—were in an area that may have suffered hits. If even one aircraft caught fire or detonated, we'd lose the lot.

I started running towards the squadron dispersal, not really knowing what purpose I could serve, but with adrenalin-fuelled legs and dust-filled eyes, covering the six hundred yards in high gear. A somewhat different version of my dash was given by the squadron duty corporal who had phoned the fire tenders for help; the duty watch mentioned seeing me weaving down the road at speed and in a manner that appeared I'd had a snootful of Scotland's best. Alas, it was not so.

At our aircraft dispersal, the situation I encountered had all the most disastrous potential that a nightmare could conjure, horrendous enough to give another case of the scours. The bombing attack was over, but two fires were blazing in the mine field not more than a hundred feet from the nearest airplane—without question the fire would rapidly spread, and we had no way of moving the aircraft in the time it would take for the blaze to close the distance (see Fig. 6).

Three airmen were feverishly bringing fire extinguishers from the aircraft and small stores building. They also had a small pile of engine cowling covers, bits of plywood, and anything flat and moveable. No one, including myself, stopped what they were doing.

"Yes sir, we called the fire tender," the man at the edge of the coiled wire managed to inform me.

The real horror was happening between forty and fifty feet *inside* the rows of wire close to the fires. My armament duty corporal had crawled over engine covers that were thrown on the barbed wire; in gaps between the covers lay bits of whatever was at hand to aid his progress. Midway from the edge of the wire and the corporal, a large airman caught fire extinguishers and hoisted them over to the corporal.

I thought—My God, I have to go in there with them. I crawled in the same path over the wire to become the third relay in feeding extinguishers to the corporal. That night providence smiled upon us, and in this lifetime of five minutes, the blaze surrounding the incendiary fires was doused

Soon after our safe retreat from the mine field, the fire tender arrived, and a few minutes after that the acting station commander appeared in his staff car, on a quick survey of the damage sites. He was a dull tool who felt a need to spread good cheer with glib witty comment, and this occasion was no exception.

"How are my boy scouts doing?"

A week later someone lost patience with his glibness—some derogatory comments dropped in the Sergeant's mess—and punched him out. There was no witness and no attempt to lay charges; the wing commander was relieved of duty two days later.

At sick bay, our doctor patched us up with bandages and a few stitches where the barbed wire had done its work. I felt a humble respect for these two young men who gave me a lesson on conduct and duty. (Unfortunately, my formal request for their commendation got lost in a screwed-up administration.) I also discovered that when moving around in a mine field, there is an unconscious attempt to levitate both feet. It was the second time in eighteen months that I'd been the unhappy occupant of a mined area; all aviators know that gravity can be an absolute killer, and mine fields only enhance that belief.

This 1942 bombing had two consequences. The first was the benefit of a stick of high-explosive bombs that landed in the Bay of Gibraltar a short way from the end of the runway extension. The detonations killed a considerable number of tasty fish, which were salvaged and served up in North Front dining halls. (We seldom had fish; I'm not sure why.) The second consequence was a fortuitous chance to put some things into proper perspective. Unknown to me, the corporal who'd been our saviour in the mine field had, on the previous Saturday, failed to be back from town in time for his scheduled night duty. His excuse and attitude hadn't been contrite enough to satisfy a work-frazzled flight sergeant, who placed the corporal "on charge" to be admonished by the squadron commander; this incident had happened two days prior to the bombing raid.

Two days after the bombing, the corporal was marched into my office, the charge of his misdemeanours read by the flight sergeant.

"Guilty or not guilty?"

"Guilty, sir." I then told him, with a stern face, "We can't have our NCOs coming in late for work, so I'm sentencing you to detached duty in England (his home). You will accompany and return with the next aircraft leaving for overhaul in the UK." The overhaul inspection usually lasted ten days. He accepted his punishment. Word of my ruthless sentence spread; it was then rumoured that some airmen were tossing lighted cigarette butts into the mine field and practising with fire extinguishers.

SUBTERFUGE AND SABOTAGE

Vichy air attacks had only a small potential to disrupt or destroy the Gibraltar supply and defence systems. However German subversive resources in Spain seemed to offer much opportunity for devising methods of destruction at North Front airfield, where well-placed explosives could have devastating results. (Again, there is no clear reason why the Germans didn't exploit this opportunity more aggressively.)

Behind-the-scenes games of espionage and counterespionage were never seen by servicemen on routine duty. But the arrest, trial, and execution of three saboteurs demonstrated the highly coordinated activities in secret agencies in the Spanish area adjacent to Gibraltar; one such unfortunate

Luis Lopez Cordon, was enticed by large rewards to carry explosives to blow up a munitions magazine.

The hundreds of Spanish men and women from La Linea and San Roque who crossed the border every day to work in Gibraltar offered an opportunity for recruitment of saboteurs and espionage agents. At the border-crossing, the checking of this daily flow of bodies appeared lax, almost casual. All of these people had considerable distances to walk to and from home and work. They knew that any significant violation of either the British or Spanish checkpoints would introduce tighter security and unneeded delays. Most of the women took home a fresh loaf of bread from Gibraltar. The significance of this prized benefit and their wages in pesetas was not to be jeopardized by harbouring any clandestine activity that held no benefit to them. The British knew this and had their own observers in the work force.

The lack of success by German agents to infiltrate Gibraltar security or inflict any significant damage on a highly visible target must be seen as a frustrating failure for the reputed 717 full-time officers and agents plus 600 part-time employees working in southern Spain.

HUMAN TORPEDOES

The third form of attack in 1942–43 was a successful series of ship minings in the Bay of Gibraltar: four supply ships were sunk, and six others moored in these protected waters were seriously damaged. In all cases, mines had been attached to the ships' hulls. This raised the urgent question: how could any enemy unit capable of the underwater attacks foil the defences and vigilance of Gibraltar Harbour and Bay protection systems?

The identity of these attackers remained a mystery until

Italy's alliance with Germany collapsed in 1943. The intriguing story that emerged has been told in various accounts of successful wartime plots; in this case, the foresight, ingenuity, and courage of Italian frogmen, skilled underwater specialists who used small, sled-like submersibles and breathing devices to infiltrate enemy harbours or moorings to destroy ships with explosives. While the Italian Navy's fleet of surface ships had not been very venturesome, these so-called "human torpedoes" had proved highly skilled and aggressive. The sinking of the British battleships *Queen Elizabeth* and *Valiant* in Alexandria Harbour, May 1941, showed commitment and an astonishing compassion: after mining both ships, the frogmen alerted the British admiral to evacuate the crews to save lives—while their own lives could be sacrificed.

Their shipping attacks in the Bay of Gibraltar had been cleverly planned, with attacks carried out from a hidden base of operation that would be undetected by both a neutral Spain and by British forces. Conchita Ramognino, the Spanish wife of an Italian officer, had a villa about two miles from Gibraltar and is credited with being one of the instigators for this concealed operation. Before Italy entered the war, it had arranged to have its merchant vessel *Olterra* docked at the Port of Algeciras, where it would be confined for the war's duration by British naval vessels in nearby Gibraltar. The *Olterra*'s immobile presence soon became a familiar, innoxious part of the landscape. But an underwater hole and water lock converted the *Olterra* into a perfect sanctuary for a team of Italians to mine nearby ships.

Seeing the result of enemy action on the proverbial doorstep within two miles of our squadrons' base—while we flew thousands of miles to protect ships at distances of four and five hundred miles —was indeed rubbing our noses in it. Nonetheless, many attacks, known and unknown, proved unsuccessful, and a spirit of defiance, a commitment to hold and protect the Rock against all attackers, was part of daily life. Gibraltar's tradition of impenetrable strength, and its survival of endless sieges in centuries of war, was for us a kind of spiritual armour and remained part of its more practical fortifications in its time as a 1940–42 outpost. And the turning point was TORCH.

CHAPTER EIGHT

THE SUMMER OF '42

THE WELLINGTON AND THE GOAT

On August 27, a radio message came in from a Wellington crew flying the Bathurst[†]-Timbuktu route to Egypt. They'd had engine failure and force landed in the Spanish Sahara desert. (A forced landing is different from a crash landing in that you still have some control of the landing; "forced" here means that there was no choice but to land.) I was detailed to try a rescue mission. Supplied with extra rations and a long-range fuel tank fitted to Hudson AE591, we took off for the last known position of the Wellington. They had reported their location as within a mile of the coast. Although they were in an area populated by nomadic Berber tribes, this was Spanish territory, where being discovered would result in a diplomatic problem or interment. And the flying time there and back would take ten or twelve hours, close to our fuel limit.

After five hours and over eight hundred miles, we found the Wellington, which had made a successful wheels-up belly landing. I started circling and communicating by Aldis lamp and Morse code. The seacoast was about a mile distant—and to my surprise and relief I saw the Royal Navy frigate moored

---

† Now Banjul, capital of The Gambia

a short way offshore. It had obviously been there a few hours;
a boat was on the beach, and the landing party had arrived at
the aircraft. They signalled a message to us:

"No injuries, any order?"

My relief came from the fact I wouldn't have to attempt
a landing, which would have been hazardous. There was a
small, dried-up, shallow waterbed about half a mile away
where, if necessary, I could attempt a soft touch-and-go
landing before any full landing commitment. With the Royal
Navy rescue at hand, I decided the risk wasn't warranted.
Besides, the extra fuel used would draw on our marginal
reserves.

"Burn and destroy leave soon," I signalled back.

"Ship wants rear gun turret."

"Take it," I signalled in response, "no long delay."

With that, we left for the return flight; our airborne time
arriving at Gibraltar was ten hours and thirty minutes, the
same flying time for crossing the Atlantic. Without a co-
pilot, that's a lengthy spell at the controls.

Two days later, I interviewed the Wellington crew, who
had returned to Gibraltar on the Royal Navy frigate. Their
story was a fascinating account of how, after a crippling
engine failure, the remaining engine was over-heating and
couldn't maintain enough power to stay airborne. They'd
wirelessed their emergency and position, and then made the
belly landing close to the sea coast, with little damage and
no injuries. Their location gave them a view of the sea that
allowed them to signal a passing ship with a red flare from
their Veri pistol.

The emergency-kit equipment and rations carried by
transient aircraft included some Spanish and French money,
with a list of useful phrases and cultural manners for dealing with the local population. Shortly after the Wellington's

emergency landing, a nomadic family of Berbers appeared, with donkeys and goats in tow, and struck camp close by. The contents of the kit now were put to use, as the crew realized that these desert dwellers were conditioned by life to be shrewd opportunists who perhaps saw before them a salvage bonanza.

The group's apparent leader seemed to know he had some bartering power but wanted a closer look at his potential prize. He showed his authority by directing women and children of various ages and sizes to stay away from the foreigners; he was the negotiator. For their part, the Wellington crew were astute enough to indicate that he and any discussions would stay well away from the aircraft. The crew knew it could be several days before they were rescued; meanwhile, water, food, and alternate plans for survival had to be considered. The following day, with sign language and a mix of Spanish and other languages, the bartering began.

A little water could be spared, at a price, and that of course wouldn't be safe to drink without including purifying tablets from the kit. There was no food to spare unless one of the small goats was slaughtered and cooked, and that would be a considerable expense. In any event, these provisions could only sustain the crew for three or four days, at which point they'd have to trek twenty-five miles over uncertain terrain to the nearest settlement. The local man was prepared to lead the way for a substantial remuneration, and as that course of action could result in Spanish internment with unpleasant incarceration, it was a plan of last resort.

The Wellington crew and the Berber finally agreed on an interim arrangement to satisfy their hunger with freshly cooked goat meat. The roasted goat that appeared that evening looked much, the crew said later, like cured leather and indeed turned out to be of that texture; no one could chew it into digestible form. The Berber was able to dispose of it at no extra charge. The Royal Navy frigate arrived the next morning.

This is one of many wartime adventures by young men improvising in emergencies that required survival in unfamiliar geographical, political, linguistic, and cultural climates. Alongside the more hazardous experiences of war lay many such occasions of nonviolent human encounter.

DINING HALL ATTACKS

Our own food rations at Gibraltar consisted of endless canned meats—mostly bully beef and stews of unknown vintage. They were at least nourishing, with Spanish fruit and vegetables occasionally lending some variety to the diet. On a few occasions, fresh beef arrived shortly after a bull fight in La Linea. Those noble animals were never meant to end up on dinner plates, and any rubber boot would have been a comparable alternative.

As warmer weather arrived, so did the flies: anyone who has tried to have a meal without contesting every bite with swarms of flies in an unscreened room has experienced the prevalent pestilence of that part of the world. Our dining hall (or, to be more accurate, the human refuelling station) was in a metal Nissen hut that gave some modest anti-fly protection, but at mealtimes masses more gained entrance. Some members of our hut decided to combat these invaders.

They formed teams of two or three people armed with rolled-paper fly swatters. About twenty minutes before mealtime, the teams would commence their attacks, carefully retaining the carcasses of each kill. The object was to have the largest number gathered by meal time, with losers buying the winners a beer. This, of course, required an impartial

FIGURE 9

The beach provided one of the few opportunities for recreation; The author (right) with Maj. Vic Odlum, Canadian Army Engineers, Gibraltar 1942

adjudicator to examine the credibility of body parts as countable; he too was entitled to a beer as payment for this judicial task. The aggressiveness of these warring aircrews was thus brought to the fore in the detection and destruction of all flying objects.

THE MAN-OF-WAR

Crew who wanted to get away from the confines of the airfield for a few hours had limited possibilities for recreation; but swimming off the eastern end of the airstrip was pleasant for those who enjoyed the water. The sandy beach was kept clean, and from early April until mid-October, temperatures were a comfortable 75° to 78° F (about 24° to 26° C). As part of my own recreation and fitness program, I made an effort to swim for an hour on days that the flight schedule and other duties permitted. On one occasion, while swimming two or three hundred feet out from the beach, my pleasure was somewhat disrupted by an encounter with a small (though I believed it giant) Portuguese man-of-war jellyfish.

I was swimming slowly, observing the sea bottom in a depth of about fifteen feet. Between breaths, my face was mostly in the water, enjoying the clear view through the anti-gas goggles I'd misappropriated from central stores. This was indeed a misuse of His Majesty's equipment, but having discovered this more civilized, improvised use of the goggles, my conscience had no trouble breaking the necessary rules.

When I struck the man-of-war, a numbing, powerful shock hit the left side of my body from neck to hip, triggering an immediate top-alarm signal to my response system and, with arms flailing at unheard-of rotation speeds, I reached the beach barely skimming the surface. Sunbathing witnesses claim that all previous world records for the hundred yards in water sports were shattered as I aquaplaned onto the beach. An angry, burning red welt on my left arm remained an open sore for weeks, with scar tissue for several years. I did continue my Gibraltar swimming exercises but decided to have no more encounters with Portuguese man-of-war.

COURT-MARTIAL:
MISADVENTURE IN LA LINEA[†]

One October morning found me in the office bent over paperwork; Command Headquarters required reports to keep the administrative wheels turning, and for me this routine paperwork was an unhappy chore. (How were wars fought before paper became so popular?)

Not all paperwork was so routine. Looking back through the distance of a half century, I reflect on a particular court-martial affair with some amusement; a time when the follies and foibles of war gave rise to stress, tragedy, and all manner of incongruous human behaviour. The following incident occurred because of the unique situation and close proximity of the Spanish towns adjoining Gibraltar, where special passes gave gullible youth fertile ground for misadventure.

On this particular morning, I was completing a serviceability and maintenance review when the adjutant interrupted my tedium to ask if I had time to chat with a Canadian sergeant of a Wellington aircraft, along with one of his crew. He added that they seemed most anxious to see me. I assumed they were probably from my hometown of

---

[†] When writing this account of the court-martial episode, I was unable to contact the persons involved to obtain their permission to use their real names in this chapter. However, these persons and events were real, and the account of the affairs in fact and detail is not embellished, the only literary license being my choice to tell this story in the first person.

Stellarton in Nova Scotia, or perhaps we had some mutual acquaintance. I said it would be a half hour if they cared to wait until I finished the review; the two let the adjutant know they wouldn't leave until I could find time to see them.

Ushering them into my office, the adjutant gave their names; neither had any personal significance. The pilot, Sergeant Broy, was a lean, fair-haired fellow of above-average height, while his air gunner, Sergeant Binns, was several inches shorter and sturdily built; they made a Mutt-and-Jeff pair. Broy, I learned, was a twenty-four-year-old bank teller from Vancouver and Binns, nineteen, a United States volunteer from Montana. Before I could ask why they were here, the conversation took a sharp turn.

"We're being court-martialled," blurted the pilot, "and we want you to be our defending officer."

There was a considerable pause. I managed a deep breath. "Why on earth did you come to me? I have no legal experience and no time to be involved, whatever your problem may be. Sorry, but you've been directed to the wrong person." I tried, without a formal dismissal, to indicate that the interview was over.

"Our trial is next week," said Binns, the younger sergeant, "and we want a Canadian to defend us. We asked other aircrew who they recommended, and they said you were our best bet."

I didn't ask what they'd done to cause their predicament and told them to keep searching. I didn't have the time or inclination to drop squadron responsibilities to sort out the problems of transient aircrew passing through Gibraltar on their way to the Middle or Far East. Two worried-looking NCOs left the office.

After lunch I walked back to my desk of paperwork to find the accused malefactors awaiting my return. They attempt-

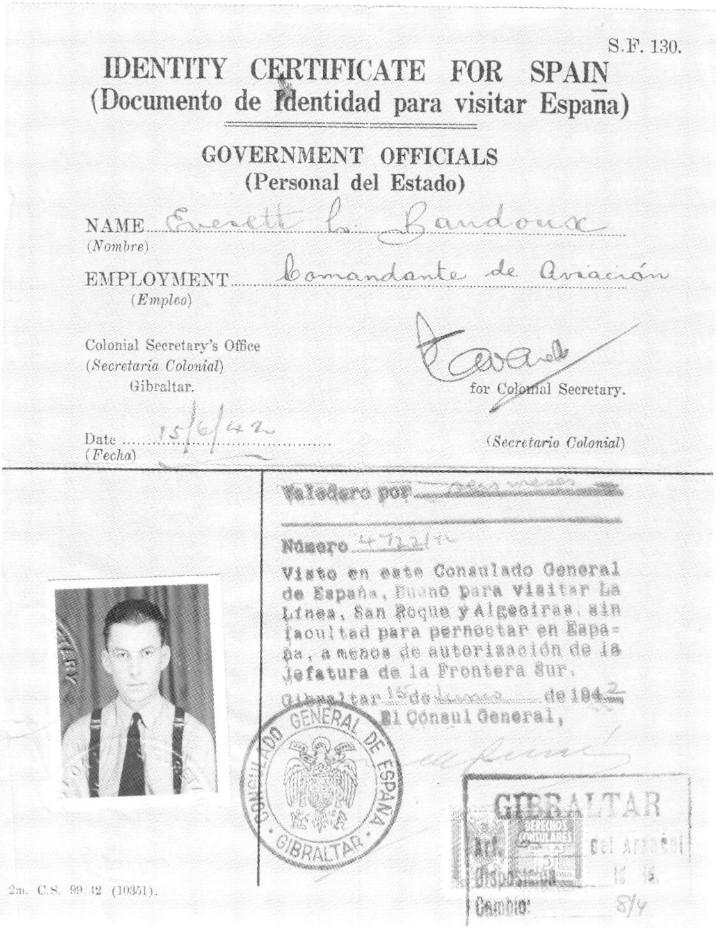

S.F. 130.

IDENTITY CERTIFICATE FOR SPAIN
(Documento de Identidad para visitar España)

GOVERNMENT OFFICIALS
(Personal del Estado)

NAME Everett L. Baudoux
(*Nombre*)

EMPLOYMENT Comandante de Aviación
(*Empleo*)

Colonial Secretary's Office
(*Secretaria Colonial*)
Gibraltar.

for Colonial Secretary.

Date 15/6/42
(*Fecha*)

(*Secretario Colonial*)

Valedero por seis meses

Número 4722/42

Visto en este Consulado General de España, Bueno para visitar La Línea, San Roque y Algeciras, sin facultad para pernoctar en España, a menos de autorización de la Jefatura de la Frontera Sur.

Gibraltar 15 de Junio de 1942

El Cónsul General,

CONSULADO GENERAL DE ESPAÑA · GIBRALTAR

GIBRALTAR

DERECHOS CONSULARES

Art. del Arancel

Disposición

Cambio: 8/4

2m. C.S. 99/42 (10351).

FIGURE 10

Passes were issued for entry to Spain. What other theater of the war had potential for such close contact with the enemy?

ed to persuade me to take up their case as an obligation of
conscience, of duty to the lower ranks, to see the plight of a
Canadian far from home. As a last, desperate measure to get
rid of them, I offered to phone the senior air administration officer to find them a competent defender. This turned
out to be a mistake; the wing commander thought I should
accept the duty, saying that a week away from flying would
be good for me, and if any urgency in squadron operations
occurred, I'd be within two miles at most. The geographic
confines of Gibraltar ensured this.

I decided to make a point of shunning the wing commander—unless he was buying the drink. Moreover, I felt
he should be prepared to shoulder the blame for further
jeopardizing the dismal prospects of these two sinners. And
so, with much reluctance, I became defending officer for
the upcoming District Court Martial. But as their story of
youthful exuberance unfolded into one of naive and dangerous bumbling[†], it looked more and more like a lost cause.

What led to the court martial began harmlessly enough.
The day after arriving at Gibraltar for refuelling and a forty-
eight-hour rest en route for Egypt, the Wellington's navigator became a victim of the local inflamed bowel syndrome
that often targeted newcomers; it left him unable to serve
as an active aircrew member for six or seven days. This left
Sergeants Broy and Binns stranded at Gibraltar, where there
was no entertainment for idle, frustrated, and vigorous young
men.

Perhaps the most dulling effect on social or community
ambience was the absence of women in everyday activities
which only amplified the atmosphere of military confine

---

†   These were just some of their characteristics; given time, they had potentia
    to make a good bomber crew.

nent. There were, of course, some women on Gibraltar, but socializing was restricted and circumspect. The female work-force from Spain was absolutely off limits, and that seemed fine with them; the women's employment allowed no free time, and the jobs were very important. Military personnel delayed at Gibraltar for more than a day or two could relieve boredom with visits to either of the local Spanish towns of Algeciras or La Linea. A special arrangement with the Spanish government allowed twelve-hour daylight passes for our servicemen to visit these restricted areas.

There, the average local Spaniard had a meagre income and wasn't inclined to be outgoing or welcoming to military strangers. Their hospitality was based on commerce, though the shopping had little to offer; consumer goods were in much greater supply and variety at Gibraltar. We didn't encourage fraternizing, and the political tensions in Spain didn't support the forming of close relationships with foreigners. So the common attractions to visiting crew were bullfights, whorehouses, and cheap wine. This is where the bored and energetic pilot and gunner started their slow sink into the military's legal quagmire.

I resigned myself to the task of defending officer and equipped myself with a thick scribbler, pencils, and a list of things to be done. In my pre-war years of officer's training, I'd sat through the required courses on Air Force Law and King's Regulations, an academic exposure to material contained in two thick volumes, and my grades had matched my interest: adequate. I'd grown even more familiar with their contents as my rank and experience increased yet was acutely aware that my knowledge of these subjects fell far short of courtroom standards. It would take an intense crash study to approach the Court with some modicum of dignity and credibility—and that didn't seem a realistic option in the time available.

I also had endless questions. The first involved a telephone call to the Judge Advocates' office in headquarters for a formal statement of the offences with which the two sergeants were charged. I discovered there were four formal charges:

1. Conduct unbecoming members of His Majesty's Forces by endangering personnel and equipment.

2. Moving an aircraft by taxying from its allotted dispersal without authorization.

3. While intoxicated behaving in a manner that caused damage to aircraft.

4. Behaving in a manner which compromised the security of military information.

Before starting my own inquiry, I obtained a copy of the military police report that detailed events leading to the sergeants' arrest. On returning from a daylight pass visit to Spain, and about twenty minutes before border closing time, my two candidates for the steel-bar hotel arrived at the gatehouse and, with what seemed to be great concentration, made a passable straight walk through the checkpoint. The Independent Company of Border Guards who controlled the British crossing into the neutral zone was well trained, observant, and perceptive. They noted the sergeants were more than moderately inebriated. They also had seen the sergeants being driven up to the Spanish gate shortly before closing for day passes; the automobile was not a known taxi—somewhat unusual, as private cars were scarce and taxis almost nonexistent in La Linea. (The significance of this was only realized later.)

The report then summarized the airfield security guards' response to an urgent call from the control tower. After nightfall, a Wellington aircraft in the transient dispersal area had started its motors and collided with a Whitley aircraft parked in the row ahead. The guards arrived at the dispersal location to encounter two very drunk sergeants emerging from a Wellington aircraft. It had come to a stop after its propellers had chewed the rear four feet of the Whitley into scrap metal. Somehow they'd managed to start both motors of the Wellington without removing the canvas covers that now were shredded into other bits of the Whitley. The report went on to say that the would-be aviators had decided it was a good night to go flying; the writer felt at liberty to add that "They were already high as a kite."

Time to get the rest of the story. The interview with my charges began and ended with no levity.

"Start at the beginning and tell me everything you did— where you were, what happened, I mean everything, with no B.S. When I ask a question, the answer has to be straight; if you lie to me or try to cover up, I'll have you locked up until someone else listens to you. Understood?"

Subdued voices answered, "Yes, Sir."

"When you went for your passes to visit La Linea, did you get the cautionary briefing about behaviour in Spain? The prosecutor at the trial will ask you this same question."

"Yes, Sir, but we didn't pay much attention," said Sergeant Broy. "We thought it was just more 'be-good-boys' stuff." The sergeant air gunner nodded his head in agreement.

"Start now and tell me everything you remember from the time you entered Spain until the security police arrested you at the airfield."

An hour later, after many questions and some painfully embarrassing answers, I was convinced that no Court was ever going to find them blameless. The whole episode was a tale of naive bravado exposed in an unfriendly or sullen society amid the acknowledged presence of enemy agents and associates. Most locals in this area of Spain were indifferent to the day pass visitors from Gibraltar and posed no physical threat (violence would have a negative impact on the small but useful visitor spending, and police action could be rigorous). The military hazards stemmed in information-gathering techniques orchestrated by German and Spanish intelligence operations, whose methods were subtle and skillful.

In a less serious time and place, the sergeants' visit had all the elements of slapstick comedy. They'd left for La Linea in the early afternoon with the intention of having a sightseeing tour, a glass or two of wine, then returning to the Rock for dinner. The only popular Spanish entertainment was the bullfighting held in the La Linea bull ring on alternate Saturdays.(These never had much appeal for our fellows; in fact, almost all who attended a bullfight were revolted and puzzled by the crowds' enthusiasm in watching an animal tortured to death.) Our wandering lads had no such chance of diversion, as the bullfights were several days away. Naturally, they gravitated to a sidewalk bistro for some liquid refreshment.

Only half the sidewalk tables were occupied, the locals ignoring the sergeants, customers drinking while watching the movement of people, most carrying parcels of sorts, a few horse-drawn carts, and an occasional motor vehicle: it was a lazy scene that kept the square in slow motion without disrupting siestas. Some youngsters kicking a tattered soccer ball, avoiding the sparse traffic, passed through the square; their skill sparked a discussion among the sergeants about favourite sports, and a comparison of American and Canadian football. During this rambling discussion of athletics and other idle chatter, between sips of sour wine and a mysterious black fluid posing as coffee, a well-dressed man in business attire, seated at an adjoining table, looked up from reading his papers.

"Pardon me," he said in a pleasantly surprised tone and good English. "Are you gentlemen from Canada?" They acknowledged that for one of them this was so; it was obvious. "Either of you, by any chance, from Winnipeg?"

"Sorry, no," they said.

"Well, you never know. My sister and her family live there—Joyce MacDonald, her husband, Jim, is in the Canadian Army."

Our fellows were careful in their response but the gent didn't seem pushy, just affable. He'd arrived at the bistro shortly after they had, drove a good-looking medium-sized French car, and was greeted by the proprietor with jovial but respectful courtesy as a person of recognized importance.

"I assume you fellows are with the military at Gibraltar," he continued. "I don't mean to pry, but I'm a British resident in Spain and thought you may like to know a bit about local points of interest."

Their conversation loosened into an amiable exchange that avoided any military content, as it gradually emerged that their new acquaintance managed British-owned vineyards and wineries near San Martin, about twenty miles from Gibraltar; the British wine holdings there, he said, were more than a century old. The conversation evolved into explanations of wine, the different types, processes, vintages, merits of the local product, and methods of determining quality and value—all fascinating to our heroes, particularly the tasting criteria. The bistro owner complied with the man's request for a specific selection of various wines, which then were generously sampled. The afternoon had become, for the sergeants, a most agreeable outing.

As an hour or so passed, our new experts on wine developed an increasing fondness for the subject. By their own admission, they were more than happily tranquillized in the acquisition of this knowledge.

Their instructor, who seems to have done more explaining and coaching than sampling, now had other appointments in the area; a business custom in the wine industry, he said, required that a senior official make periodic courtesy calls on local distributors. After explaining his need to depart, he paused. Then asked, as what seemed like an afterthought, if they'd care to accompany him to some of the establishments. Part of this tour would involve discussion and sampling of the wares. The sergeants readily took up this invitation. A few convivial stops were formalized with a glass or so, amid mostly Spanish with a smattering of English chatter, understood by the sergeants to be an exchange of pleasantries.

As the afternoon advanced, their memory and discretion retreated. I did manage to get the air gunner to admit, with reluctance and great embarrassment, their visit to a building that housed a "social club", according to their new mentor. Their greeting by the female "manager" was more than friendly as she introduced several of her younger assistants, also female. One of these charmers spoke considerable English and took an immediate passion to our air gunner. She was crazy, she said, about strong, handsome Americans. How brave they were, she said; he and she would talk and become better acquainted in her room. She was a very inquisitive and imaginative entertainer; the sergeant left the rest to my understanding. I didn't need any details except to know if their "private talk" included military queries. He acknowledged they had, but said he didn't have answers.

That about summarizes their visit in Spain. Once back in Gibraltar with their bravado well fuelled and maintained by a gift bottle, the two sergeants were ready to challenge the world. Night had fallen, and a full moon mixed light and shadows on the lines of aircraft. What better way for these skilled and daring aviators to complete their day than to crank up the 'Wimpey' and go for a flight.

Neither recalled who proposed the idea to go night flying, though finding the aircraft and getting both motors started was, at the very least, a remarkable feat for which they could give no account. At the end of this tale of misadventure, my exasperation was tempered with a twinge of sympathy for a couple of small-town guys who had just encountered the real world. I told them what they must have hated to hear:

"You fellows have had the dubious pleasure of being royally entertained by a German agent, and you ended up by helping the enemy in severely damaging two of our aircraft. I have a lot of unproductive work to do to try to keep you in the war on our side. Be here tomorrow at 1300."

In retrospect, I should have left the rebuke until much later in the pretrial efforts, but they had to prepare for a real scathing or prison; this was not a winnable case. Discovering how to mitigate the damage and plead clemency seemed the only option.

The next morning I met Flight Lieutenant Monty Riddell, the airfield control officer; I sought an unbiased account of the Wellington colliding with the Whitley. Monty was a tough-love type, an excellent officer, and everyone respected his competent steady manner in handling a difficult job. Looking after crashes and squeezing large airport operations into Gibraltar's restricted space was an unusual challenge. He described the events in typical point-blank fashion.

"Those two fellows were pissed out of their minds. How they fired up the Wimpey is incredible."

Unfortunately, the Whitley damage was real trouble. That particular aircraft had been sent over from the UK with the latest bad-weather instrument landing equipment, to assure all-weather transportation for high-level VIP War Office nobs. One such VIP, on hearing about the Whitley damage, was advocating the perpetrators be shot.

The good news was that our engineering officer, with his usual ingenuity, was replacing the damaged tail section with parts borrowed from another Whitley waiting for engine repair. The damaged aircraft, he said, should be serviceable by the afternoon; this could be useful in reducing the consequences of the drunken conduct charge.

I felt gratitude for the resourceful and skillful work performed by the North Front Aircraft Repair and Maintenance Unit; they were high on my list of unsung heroes. Day after day, they salvaged and fixed aircraft damaged in the landing mishaps that seemed endemic for the transient and inexperienced pilots now regularly arriving on the short North Front runway.

The more I considered the sergeant's circumstances and the evidence that would be presented at trial, the more I became convinced that an acquittal was not even a remote possibility. My challenge was to present some appeal for clemency, for a tempering of sentence that would satisfy the disciplinary code while not removing Broy and Binns from the war effort.

There wasn't time to ponder any subtle ploy or to learn any greater courtroom competence, so a friendly talk with the Judge Advocate office seemed the most direct way to sound things out. At any rate, it couldn't do any harm.

I arranged a late-morning meeting with the senior advocate, Squadron Leader Trevor Jones.[†] I needed no more than two minutes to know that I had the good fortune to be dealing with a quality human. The Squadron Leader was a man in his mid forties, with slightly greying hair on top of an athletic frame and an easy, friendly manner devoid of any adversarial barriers.

"I recall we met at the Governor's cocktail party about a month ago," he said. "Will you have a cup of tea with me?"

I affirmed both comments, though I wondered how this man remembered a cursory introduction among a hundred others at the Monastery[‡] party.

"You no doubt know I've been given the chore of defending officer for two sergeants at the court martial next Wednesday?" I didn't want to sound like a supplicant, and he immediately put me at ease without any tinge of official reticence. Looking at the intelligent eyes of a real professional, I decided to put my concerns to him in a forthright way and see what he could offer to ease my dilemma.

"I came to see you," I began, "because the facts and circumstances as now known do not leave much doubt about the mess these two NCOs have got themselves into. I certainly am not qualified to defend them and have told them so. This leaves me in the position of explaining and advising what I believe to be in the best interest of the Service and asking for as much compassion as rational judgement can

---

† Name changed.
‡ The residence of the Governor of Gibraltar.

allow. The nature of the offences was not malicious, subversive, or contrived. The point I find difficult is in having to face the expertise of a professional lawyer prosecuting the accused in arguments of law, while I, an untrained novice, am advocating some kind of tolerance for youth and inexperience; it hardly seems like a fair contest. Is there any middle ground?"

With the barest hint of a smile, he told me not to think of it as a contest, that we present the known facts and relate them to the charges. The information is there for the Court to form opinion and make judgements. If the information isn't supported by witnessed fact and evidence that should be discerned by a normally perceptive person; no harm should come from challenging a charge not supported by law or fact. Argument about meaning or interpretation of law is usually distracting and unproductive. Simplicity is generally best. Our purpose is not to prosecute but to help keep the service functioning by using law and order to support discipline.

I thanked him and headed back to the squadron office. I liked the man; he had been helpful and, unless I misunderstood his comments, they were not after blood but wanted to enforce good order.

By 1300 hours, having recovered from the mess hall lunch, I made some notes on a proposed line of defence and supplication to the court martial. The complete procedure and deportment in the trial would have to be thoroughly understood by the sergeants, who'd need to be in agreement with our proposed handling of the charges. Sergeant Broy, the pilot, was waiting in the adjoining adjutant's office, but there was no sign of Sergeant Binns.

I was about to voice my irritation at this disregard of my instructions when the telephone rang. The adjutant put his head through the open door.

"Sir, Captain George of the Independent Company Border Guard, he wants to speak with you."

I took the phone. "Yes, Captain. What can I do for you?"

His answer completed a now thoroughly spoiled lunch. "I have a Sergeant Binns, aircrew gunner, detained here. He tells me he's responsible to your command. We stopped him from going into Spain on a day pass; he was carrying a loaded Smith and Weston .38 pistol. I have no need for more lock-ups. What do you want done with him?"

Ten seconds, twenty seconds of silence passed; my mind scrambled to get back on track. My first unspoken thought was—Dear God, the kid must be short of a full deck!

"Sir?" said Captain George.

"Could you have an escort deliver him to our squadron office—separated from his gun?"

"My pleasure," said the captain, "and by the way, we kept his day pass."

I thanked Captain George and, still dumbfounded, asked myself how we could have been so bloody stupid as to leave those fellows with passes. The control system for passes had a hole to be plugged forthwith; the adjutant would take care of that problem.

While waiting for the arrival of our wayward air gunner, I had Sergeant Broy come into the office, told him what had happened, and asked if he had any explanation.

"Sir, I had no idea what he was thinking," he blurted, obviously alarmed. "What will this do to us?"

I replied that if new charges resulted, it certainly would not help, and that I'd speak to Sergeant Binns alone. Meanwhile, he should remain in the adjutant's office.

"Sir, military security escort is here with Sergeant Binns. Shall we send him in?"

I asked if the sergeant's gun was locked up, and if there were any new charges against him. The adjutant said that the security unit captain had left the matter to my discretion. With some relief, I told him to express my thanks to the captain and to send in Sergeant Binns and no one else.

The door shut behind Sergeant Binns, who saluted and stood as still as possible. I could see a tremble in his legs; this kid was scared, ashamed, and alone. The military ethic was to treat him like a man, yet he hadn't quite arrived there. A few were old at nineteen; most were young but aged fast on operation—if they survived. Air Gunner Binns needed some help to cope with the hard world he was now part of. I decided he had some character qualities that deserved a gentle rescue; he had gumption, commitment, and was action oriented. His wisdom and discretion, though, were in need of considerable growth.

"What's your name, sergeant?"

Somewhat bewildered, he answered "Binns, Sir."

"No, I mean your first name."

"Chancey, Sir."

"Take off your cap and sit down, Chancey. We're going to have a very serious talk, just between you and me."

There were only two hard, metal chairs in the small and sparsely furnished office. "Place your chair in front of me and then tell me what you had in mind trying to enter Spain with a loaded revolver."

He hesitated. "I was going to kill him."

"Who? The man who was your friendly companion in La Linea?"

"Yes, Sir. After what you had said, I realized he was a German agent who used us and caused us to damage the aircraft. I felt responsible to even the score."

This lad was not by any stretch a deep thinker. "We'll talk

about that later, but now I want to discuss why you're here. Tell me, why did you join the Royal Canadian Air Force?"

"I guess it was to fight some Germans."

"Chancey, unless you had some good reason to hate German people, that is not a good answer. Give me another reason."

He looked like he had been caught playing hookey from school. "Seemed like an exciting thing to do, fighting in the air. People would be proud of me helping to win the war."

I nodded my approval. "Yes, that's what motivates many, if not most, who become aircrew. But it's a dangerous adventure that can only be made less dangerous by acquiring self-discipline and responsibility—they go hand in hand. Your companions and crewmembers depend on you when your lives are at stake. They don't need an impulsive, irresponsible character as part of their team. People in the Air Force have a tradition of looking after and caring about each other. I'm trying to do that right now."

"Let me tell you about the possible and likely consequence of your attempt to get into Spain," I continued. "If by chance you had got past the border security with a loaded gun, several things, all most unpleasant, could happen. And none of them would have resulted in anything useful in correcting your past mistake.

"First, if the Spanish police found you with a gun, you'd end up in a grim Spanish prison for a considerable time. We'd lose a valuable, expensively trained air gunner aircrew from the war effort. Second, there is no possibility that you could revisit the bistro or other locations without being noticed, and word of your presence would be passed along the network of informants. Third, the enemy agent you intended to encounter knows you are of no value now and would report you to the police. They, in turn, would have no problem finding a reason to pick you up. Fourth, if by the remotest chance you encountered the agent—who, by the way, was simply doing his job—and you shot the fellow, he would be replaced and you most likely would end up being hung. Again, we lose a valuable, expensively trained air gunner to help win the war."

Sergeant Binns was having some difficulty in holding back tears.

"Chancey, do you know what I've been telling you about responsibility to yourself and others? If so, I want your solemn word that there will be no more disruptions in our affairs. We all make mistakes. It's what we do next that's most important."

"Yes, Sir. Thank you, Sir."

"Thanks will be in your future conduct and performance. Replace your headgear, then wait with Sergeant Broy."

With a salute and smart about-turn, Chancey Binns replaced his headgear and left the office. For some reason I smiled. Only when on trial did offenders remove their forage caps.

After a short break, the sergeants were called back into the office to review their four charges and to finalize our defence. I told them it was hopeless to attempt to argue the first charge (endangering personnel and equipment, and conduct unbecoming), that a major fire and disastrous explosion could have resulted from their actions, and that there were no mitigating circumstances. If we attempted to argue a "not guilty" plea, the Court would likely believe that the accused weren't accepting responsibility or did not regret their actions, which could result in a harsh, career-ending sentence. The same reasoning applied to charge number three (intoxication causing aircraft damage): this charge was based on specific, documented fact and they should plead "guilty."

However, on charges two and four—moving aircraft without authorization, and compromising security of military information—it was possible to enter a "not guilty" plea, as Air Force Law and King's Regulations didn't contain a clear basis for these charges. The point of question in charge two was that there existed no provision for authorization to move an aircraft on the ground.

The two sergeants took full responsibility for accepting the pleas as discussed. I then gave them a stern set of instructions on courtroom attitude and deportment:

"Be at the HQ administration offices one hour before trial time. Be immaculate and maintain a good posture, military bearing. Be attentive to everything said and respectful in anything you say or do. Be absolutely honest, and answer only what is asked."

I'd written down these four points. "Read them over several times and again on the morning before the trial. Your good records will be given with a sincere supplication to the Court to permit your continued service as a trained bomber crew. The trial commences at 0930, day after tomorrow. Unless you have some further information or questions, we'll meet before the trial on Wednesday morning."

The morning of the court-martial trial, I found myself in a room normally used for lectures and training, with none of the usual trappings to dignify the process of justice. The room was pleasantly cool, and sunlight shone through large windows along one side. The setting and atmosphere was more like that of a military briefing—not intimidating, just a typical military administration area. Tables and chairs had been set up temporarily for the three members of the

Court, their legal advisor and recording clerk at one end, with defence, accused, prosecution, and observers facing the Court. Witnesses remained outside until called.

I felt relaxed. After setting my briefing notes on the defence table in order, I spent ten minutes before the commencement talking to Sergeants Broy and Binns. There was nothing to discuss; they were well groomed, and my purpose now was to try to get the wooden look of apprehension off their faces. This entire unhappy experience was not nearly as perilous for them as attacking low-level targets or enemy defences; however they didn't know this, and self-recrimination is wounding in its own way.

Squadron Leader Trevor Jones took his seat at the prosecution table. He certainly had all the assurance that comes with courtroom familiarity. I nodded to him as a courtesy of recognition; he, with a faint smile, mouthed "Good luck." It was not facetious.

All rose, the Court assembled, with a wing commander as president, and a squadron leader and flight lieutenant as members. The wing commander and flight lieutenant were general list flying types; the squadron leader was administration list. (I knew two of the Court members slightly, but I wasn't aware of any personal influence, or a bias such as attributing undisciplined behaviour as a "colonial characteristic.")

The Court opened with routine procedure: identifying the accused, reading charges, and entering pleas in response to the charges. Then came my time to speak.

"President and members of the Court, as the accused sergeants on trial have been jointly charged with all the same offences, I would ask the Court to accept that the pleas and all comments made by the defence be applicable equally to both defendants. I am unaware if this is an abnormal procedure, but as both defendants have agreed to their equal responsibility, the procedure would be abbreviated without compromise by so doing."

The President asked the prosecution if he concurred with the defence's proposal. Jones' response was that, with the Court's acceptance, he would be in agreement. The Court accepted.

I continued.

"President, the four charges having been read, once again with the Court's permission and in the interest of expediency, the defence wishes now to enter pleas and to argue the pleas collectively or individually, as you direct.

"The defendants plead 'guilty' to charge one: conduct unbecoming members of His Majesty's Forces by endangering personnel and equipment. Also guilty to charge three: while intoxicated behaving in a manner that caused damage to His Majesty's aircraft.

"The defendants plead 'not guilty' to charge two: moving an aircraft by taxying from its allotted dispersal without authorization. Also 'not guilty' to charge four: behaving in a manner which compromised the security of military information."

The prosecution accepted the guilty pleas but made available to the Court a brief of their own and reports detailing the severity of these offences.

President: "Would the prosecution now proceed with charge number two?"

Squadron Leader Trevor Jones began his address to the Court by describing the sequence of events leading up to the sergeants' arrest; he presented the police reports and the technical reports of aircraft damage, with authors and witnesses of the documents available to the Court to give sworn evidence if required. Jones then advised that no redress exist-

ed to excuse the NCOs state of intoxication for the breach of
authorization and equipment control procedures that were
long-established practices in operating military equipment
in general and aircraft in particular.

The fact, he said, that the defendants acknowledged an
unacceptable degree of intoxicated incompetence does not
mitigate the act of moving the aircraft for an unauthorized
purpose, and it violates basic safeguard principles. When an
aircraft is to be moved, for any appropriate reason, direction
is given to do so by an officer or NCO having the responsibility and authority to make that decision. Some exception may
occur when an emergency could possibly warrant the movement of aircraft without the normal authorization routine;
however, in this instance no emergency existed. In moving
the aircraft without any authorization, none of the protective
systems were present: no ground crew, no fire extinguishers,
no wheel checks—the list of violations ignored practically
every published safety manual on the operation of aircraft.
These NCOs, in taking onto themselves the authority to use a
very valuable property of His Majesty for their own purpose,
breached a most essential authorization control procedure.
No matter what the circumstance, such misconduct cannot
be ignored or left unpunished. Jones concluded by asking the
Court to find the accused guilty as charged.

President: "Defending officer, would you now address the
Court on the charge as specified?"

I was uneasy about introducing a technical argument
which might be construed as a lack of remorse by the defendants or give the Court an impression that I was pretentious
in assuming the role of legal nit-picker. Humility and sincerity were in this instance my natural allies. I was brief.

"If it pleases the Court, the defence requests the withdrawal of charge number two. The charge alleges an offence in

unauthorized movement or taxying an aircraft. We have been unable to find any law or regulation that specifically requires a formal authorization to move aircraft on the ground, other than technical qualifications to operate the equipment. The controls normally used in marshalling or parking aircraft are by radio and/or by hand signals. Details of authorization are not given; there are apparently no regulations. Therefore any supposed breach or violation is in supposition or interpretation of accepted practice and is not entrenched in formal documented regulation. It is the defences' view that the substance and intent of charge number two is already embodied in charges one and three—to which the defendants have entered a plea of 'guilty'. Charge number two is submitted to be without proper foundation and redundant. A dismissal or withdrawal of the charge is requested."

President: "A rebuttal or summary statement may be made by the prosecution on completion of all the charges being heard. Meanwhile, the technical validity of charge two, as challenged by the defence, will be reviewed by staff during the midday adjournment. Would the prosecution now proceed to charge number four?"

Trevor Jones again commenced. "The charge deals with the serious matter of violation of security," he said. "As the Court realises, the unique position of Gibraltar in the close proximity of the Spanish border creates a need for a very high and rigourously enforced standard of security. The presence of enemy agents and informants less than a mile from the North Front airfield is a constant threat to the protection of classified information. We give specific briefings and take other measures to alert our personnel to this hazard.

"One such briefing is standard procedure for servicemen who apply for visit passes to the local Spanish towns of Algeciras and La Linea. These point out the type of problems that may be encountered and caution day-pass visitors to avoid all political and military topics. Visitors are also warned about over-friendly casual acquaintances and told to be wary of argumentative or compromising situations.

"Evidence contained in the formal inquiry of the charge before the Court clearly substantiates that the accused had ignored the security briefing, and in an irresponsible state of drunkenness were incapable of discretion or guarding military information. Moreover, they were seen getting out of an automobile believed to be that of an informant or enemy agent." With that, Jones concluded:

"The Court is requested to find the defendants guilty of conduct that breaches the maintenance of security and classified information."

President: "Defending officer, please give your position for the accused."

"The defence has not called witnesses to give testimony because all evidence pertaining to the actual offences occurred within the confines of the North Front Station, and it is a matter of record that the defence accepts such evidence to be accurate and unbiased."

"With reference to what may have occurred in Spain, there is only conjecture and supposition. The only evidence that could be given would be that of the accused sergeants, and they believe sincerely that, despite their state of inebriation, they remained conscious of the need to refrain from any military or political conversation. I ask the Court to believe them. As a somewhat perverse example of their mental capacity, they demonstrated the ability to access and start the motors of a Wellington aircraft, so it is not unreasonable that they also retained and maintained an awareness of protecting security violation."

"The supposition of the prosecution is that a potential for security violation existed, therefore such an offence occurred. That premise does not sustain the basis of the charge. In a practical assessment, the unintentional divulgence of any information unknown to the enemy is indeed remote, as neither of the accused have any significant knowledge that would be new or unique to the enemy. We all are aware that movements of aircraft and ships are openly visible to enemy agents. The Wellington crew have no knowledge of other aircraft movements or their own destination until given their departure briefing. The defence submits that there has been no breach of security and no evidence of any such violations."

Time had passed quickly, the proceedings brief. Court members indicated their intention of reading the prosecution's summary on charges where a guilty plea had been offered. There was also the matter of reviewing legal technicality about charge two, authorization of a moving aircraft. At 1100 hours the President called a twenty-minute recess, instructing both prosecution and defence to be ready for their final summaries when the Court reconvened.

At 1120 hours, Squadron Leader Jones presented his summation:

"Honourable Sirs, the facts of the charges against the accused have been well and truly established both by documented evidence in the formal inquiry and admission of culpability in the guilty pleas for charges one and three. The degree of severity of damage resulting from their totally irresponsible activity is not only very substantial but casts doubt on their character fitness as members of aircrew. It would seem they may not have an understanding of the efforts and sacrifice that have been made to train them and to build the aircraft with which they have been entrusted to help defeat the enemy. The Court must make it clear to them that they have not honoured that trust.

"With regard to charge number two, that of unauthorized operation of an aircraft, the prosecution is of the opinion that, although explicit and detailed authorization may not, in every conceivable situation, be contained in regulations or operating orders, it nevertheless is implicit that the operation of any mobile equipment or similar sophisticated machinery of His Majesty's Government cannot be casually used for personal gratification without any permission whatsoever. However, if the Court determines there is technical uncertainty in the form of required authorization, the prosecution can agree to the substance of charge two being considered as germane to the guilty in charge one.

"The reason for charge number four is indeed pertinent and important. It stems from a blatant disregard of important warnings given in the briefing for day-pass visitors to Spain. The accused were told that personal danger was not a problem, but that other hazards were present; they obviously paid little or no attention. This attitude in areas of enemy presence, either on the ground or in the air, is unacceptable. Their total behaviour violated the purpose of security warnings and instructions. The basis of the charge is warranted and valid."

With that, the prosecution completed its case and left the floor to a novice defending officer who was experiencing a growing sense of inadequacy. To me, the prosecution's presentation was succinct and compelling. The whole case had been brief and without confusing controversy on fact, admissibility of views, and whatever I'd thought to be usual; also, the members of the Court appeared satisfied. There had been a few questions—"Was the night of the incident dark?"

for example, or "Is access to the dispersal unit guarded?" "Was there any medical examination or medical opinion on the degree of intoxication of the accused?" These queries by the Court were fielded by Squadron Leader Jones from his notes. (Myself, I did not see any relevant purpose to the questions.)

President: Will the defence now give its summation?"

"If it pleases the Court, what I have to say is more of an explanation and supplication than a summation. The defence cannot and has no wish to refute the evidence that has been placed before it; however, where there is no evidence of misdeeds, it asks that the supposition and probability of an offence be ignored and the accused found not guilty.

"There is no doubt about the occurrence that resulted in charges one and three, to which the accused have pleaded guilty. The sergeants insist that I tell the Court that their gross aberration of conduct has caused them an agony of remorse. They also expressed concern that other transient aircrew visiting Spain be more rigourously made aware of the type of situation for which they themselves were unprepared. The intent of this comment is not to imply that the security briefing for visiting Spain is lacking appropriate warnings but—as with most repetitive or routine procedures—the formality loses impact and the importance of the message is somewhat diminished. The accused suffered a failure of attentiveness in that respect.

"Quite likely, Gibraltar is the only location in the world where a major, strategically important military installation is within one mile of a town in a bordering neutral country that allows agents to operate with impunity and contrary to military protocol, where military personnel of a warring nation are permitted casual access. This is surely unique!"

"In this strange and unfamiliar environment of clandestine enemy activities, a casual and naive visitor is not likely to be on even terms with trained experienced agents who are well practiced in a subtle form of warfare."

"It is assumed that the defendants may have encountered one of our neighbouring enemies, who we believe failed to glean any military information but who succeeded in inflicting considerable damage by getting them drunk. I submit this explanation is highly probable and not intended to suggest exclusion, but human mistakes take many forms and the measure of acceptance should allow for all contributing circumstances."

"Sergeants Broy and Binns joined the Royal Canadian Air Force as volunteers. Their individual records are exemplary, and as aircrew their team sprit, enthusiasm, and strong motivation for joining an operational unit is testimony of their commitment to their duty. They do not expect to be lightly admonished for their serious lapse in disciplined behaviour, and irresponsible conduct will not be in their future."

"I submit to the Court that the crew of Sergeants Broy and Binns is a valuable and competent asset of our bomber force. I request that—within the bounds of the Court's discretion of good order and discipline—they be returned to duty. I thank the Court for its tolerance in allowing me to present the defence without the precision of experienced counsel; I trust it has been useful in your deliberation."

President: "Thank you, defending officer. The Court is now adjourned until 1430 hours this afternoon."

Squadron Leader Trevor Jones had his usual faint smile when he beckoned me with a nod; I went over to the table.

"That wasn't too bad, was it?" he said. "Let's go and have lunch."

"What about the trial?"

"Our job is over, but we can't discuss it until the Court is dismissed. That's the rule."

Lunch here was a notch above that of the average North Front dining standard; Headquarters mess had purloined the best chef in the Command. It was also an unexpected and pleasant respite from the week's work. Most of my squadron duties had been delegated to Flight Lieutenant Harvey, but I'd flown a five-hour sortie on a guard patrol to protect Force H, made necessary by a pilot shortage—more victims of the local gut ailment which afflicted without discrimination, and which, striking a transient Wellington crew member, had left Broy and Binns with so much free time.

While at lunch, Squadron Leader Jones diverted our thoughts away from the trial; he had a way of making every topic of chit-chat interesting. One of his queries concerned my remaining time at Gibraltar and subsequent activities. I explained that I'd already flown a hundred hours more than the normal rotation limit of five hundred, due to the loss of Squadron Leader Waddington and crew shortly after his arrival as my replacement. Waddington was the second squadron leader designated to be my relief who didn't survive long enough to allow my departure. My own survival would be rewarded on return to Scotland, where I and my bride-to-be, Daphne Mary Gilmour, were to make our wedding vows. I was in love. Moreover, her mother, Lady Violet Gilmour, had published the bans in Largo Church, and I had best be there!

Near the end of lunch, Trevor Jones gave me the address of his London law firm, which would know his whereabouts; it was an invitation to lunch at his club. A year later, I was able to take the opportunity to meet there with him—another pleasant occasion. I learned, from other sources, that my brief military legal experience had been alongside a most courteous gentleman who also happened to be a senior and prominent criminal lawyer.

At 1430 hours the Court reconvened, and the President announced that decisions had been made and that their findings and judgements would now be given.

President: "Will the defending officer and the accused now rise. The findings are: On charges one and three, the pleas of 'guilty' are accepted and confirmed. Charge number two is withdrawn because the interpretation and ambiguity of the regulations pertaining to moving on-the-ground aircraft do not give a clear basis for the charge. On charge number four, the accused are found 'not guilty.' The Court indicated that this verdict is the only one that can be given but that the Scottish verdict of 'not proven' could have been appropriate if it were legal in military jurisdiction. It is the judgement of the Court that the accused are sentenced as follows:

"Each is to pay a fine of two months wages. Each will lose two months seniority. Each will be recorded with a severe reprimand. Neither will be promoted for one year. These findings and judgements will be submitted to the Air Officer Commanding for confirmation. The Court is now dismissed."

Two days later, Sergeants Broy and Binns arrived at the 233 Squadron office. When these two sergeants left my untender care, it was the last I saw of them (whether they survived the war or are still alive, I do not know). Their aircraft and crew was departing for Egypt via the West Africa-Khartoum route. They thanked me; I thought they'd both aged somewhat but otherwise looked happy. And the war went on.

CHAPTER NINE

DEATH &
COURTESY

North Front, September 13: three days since one of our aircraft was seen plunging into the sea. The Spanish fishing vessel that recovered all four crew bodies reported that the aircraft was on fire when it hit the water in an apparent semi-controlled crash. Nobody had any explanation for the crash; any technical or crew failure that would result in an onboard fire was extremely remote, and there was no known precedent for such an occurrence in a Hudson aircraft. The report of what the fisherman had witnessed was vague, and there had been no wireless transmission from the aircraft to indicate any emergency or combat activity. They'd been flying in an area that had seen encounters with Vichy French fighters; this probability lurked in my mind, but without any evidence my speculations remained just that.

I did feel sure that the crash was caused by an external source. I always instructed my own crew gunners to fire without hesitation on any unknown aircraft approaching in the rear quadrant. Waddington, though, had only been with the squadron for five weeks and didn't share my wariness of the Vichy Navy fighters that operated out of Port Lyautey (Kenitra). His crew of Pilot Officer Johnson, Flight Sergeant Kenyon, and Sergeant Moore were all familiar with Gibraltar operations, and Squadron Leader Waddington was himself an old hand in the RAF, three years older than myself and well suited to command our squadron.

As I took in the news of Waddington's crash, my thoughts weren't entirely caught up in crew loss but also concerned with the effect of accident, illness, and disruption in an endemic alternation of hands-on command. The fractured deployment of 233 Squadron from the UK in early 1942 had been a clumsy arrangement, in which half the aircraft and crew were dispatched to Gibraltar. I was the deputy Squadron Commander and Flight Commander of the detachment of eight aircraft. The rest of aircraft and crews, with the Officer Commanding, remained at RAF Thorney Island in England. This situation of remote command control at a distance of 1,100 miles was (at best) functionally awkward. It also left some of the squadron in comfortable quarters in the UK while those at North Front, Gibraltar were living in shipping crates.

When I'd rejoined 233 Squadron in April 1942, Terry McComb—deputy Squadron Command for several months in late '41—was promoted to replace the previous Officer Commanding (OC). McComb, like me, had had an earlier tour on 233 Squadron in 1940 as a junior officer; he was an affable man who didn't favour heavy-handed discipline. He leaned toward morale building with patience and fairness that made for a good working rapport with crews and servicemen. I'd never flown with McComb, though he'd once flown with me in a Beaufighter. I had reason to believe that he didn't see his role as an aggressive "into-battle" style of leader; still, he flew patrols when his other duties allowed.

The UK portion of 233 Squadron was sent to join the Gibraltar crews in May, with everyone committed to the same heavy workload on the same rations. From May to July, McComb was back and forth to England for official reasons; on these extended occasions I'd manage his OC's duties as well as flying my regular schedule. When Waddington arrived at the end of July, McComb was on sick leave, and I was relieved that a more senior squadron leader was at hand to attend to the squadron commander's duties.

We assumed that a change of command would take place at the end of September, with Terry Waddington replacing Terry McComb, who'd be tour expired.[†] And I'd hopefully assumed that with the new replacement, 233 Squadron's command structure would stabilize—at least to a normal wartime level of personnel departure and replacement.

Now Waddington was lost. And on this September morning I was a 23-year-old looking into the future after five months of active war duty filled with that strange mix of uncertainty and natural optimism. But it was always difficult to rationalize the sacrifice of young lives, to accept these losses with the conviction that each new day was to be met with a commitment for winning the war.

When the phone rang, the caller identified himself as the senior intelligence officer at Gibraltar HQ. He'd had communication from the local Spanish naval authority that they'd recovered the Waddington crew bodies and were prepared to transport these to us on a torpedo launch. This was a military courtesy that exceeded our expectations, and we immediately received the Governor's approval to dock a foreign navy vessel at the North Moles at 1400 hours.

The North Mole lay outside the sheltering walls of the enclosed harbour and was normally used for commercial traffic. My assignment was to arrange appropriate personnel

---

[†] In the end, McComb's tour as OC did expire September 30; I once again took command until Wing Commander Devey was appointed and arrived a month later. I, too, was nearing the number of operational hours for transfer to other duties, but crew losses and the demand for increased sorties and patrols required that I remain until mid-February '43, at which time I'd exceeded the tour requirement by almost two hundred hours.

and vehicles to meet the Spanish craft with an expression of our appreciation. Then came the fly in the ointment: the intelligence chief went on to explain that the commander who'd be the launch captain was not, in fact, its regular skipper but a temporary replacement, identified as someone with connections to German agents.

I decided to be at the Mole well in advance of the scheduled docking. Attired in my best clean uniform and with three cartons of State Express cigarettes for the launch crew, I arrived at the appointed location a half hour early. The transport lorry was freshly washed, and the six airmen in summer dress would pass parade inspection. Tied to the dock were two small vessels about a thousand tons each and separated by about 150 feet. I didn't know the length or size of the arriving torpedo boat and simply took for granted that this location and the technicalities of docking were cleared by whoever managed the North Mole.

As we waited, four Gibraltarian longshoremen sat on a bench beside the main building facing the docking area, some sixty or eighty feet back. These gentlemen obviously knew that something out of the ordinary was expected; it was equally obvious that there was nothing more important to occupy them than local observance, vocal deliberations, and smoking. This was their territory, and all others were interlopers to be scanned and derided. Outsiders who ventured to the loading area referred to these locals as "Rock scorpions"; abrasive, independent, and tough, their nickname was granted to them at least in part for the loud hissing sound they made to attract one another (whether a disparagement or greeting, they alone knew; I had no desire to find out).

The launch arrived as scheduled, with four plain wooden coffins on the middle deck. I would remain emotionally aloof to show that we accepted death as a commitment to our duty. Still, looking at the rough boxes, I was once again reminded that the price was high. Waddington was the only son of a widowed mother, and kin of the other deceased crew members would be wracked with similar grief.

After the launch crew fastened lines to the Mole and placed a gangway ashore, the boat commander walked to where I was standing and saluted. I immediately returned his salute, then, as intelligence briefing had suggested as accepted protocol, extended my hand in a diplomatic handshake.

"I am Lieutenant Commander M———"[†] he said, in good English. "It is my duty with full respect to return to you the bodies of your squadron, recovered from the water by one of our fishing boats." His delivery of these first few words sounded stiff, rehearsed, cool, and formal. He had blue eyes and a stature much larger than was usual for Spanish males—we were about the same height and build—though I've been told that his fair complexion and physique was not uncommon in some Spanish families. I sensed that nothing here would extend beyond the courtesies of the occasion.

Crew carried the coffins from the boat to the Mole, where my six airmen stood in line to place them in the covered lorry. I saluted each coffin in turn. The Spanish Lieutenant Commander made a comment to the effect that 'those who die in the service of their cause must be honoured'. I tried to respond in a similar vein, something like 'In the military profession, we all give respect to valour and sacrifice'. I then offered my official thanks to him and his crew for their act of courtesy and compassion and produced the cartons of cigarettes that I hoped his crew would accept as a small token of

---

[†] Name not Known

appreciation. There'd be another salute as they cast off the lines, and we could leave. Or so I thought.

Alas, the space between the two vessels, where the torpedo launch had docked, was too confined for the helmsman to make a graceful departure against the stiff breeze holding it to the Mole. The next five minutes of the launch nudging and rubbing the other ships resulted in three failed attempts to get the nose of the launch pointed outward; I solemnly saluted each promising departure. The Rock scorpions were delighted with the show. They stayed stuck to their bench, expressing their opinion of what they were witnessing in little hand gestures and knowing facial expressions. Our uninvited audience's contemptuous behaviour was not unnoticed by the frustrated, exasperated launch commander, who was puce with restrained anger at being mocked by these practised experts. His fourth attempt to leave was successful on my last salute.

Two days later, we interred the four bodies in the Gibraltar cemetery, where they lay with others who, in this conflict on the road to peace, had left life's journey all too soon.

OCTOBER'S BITTER LOSS

Being alert to the ever-present danger on all sorties was always a mental discipline for my crew, but humans aren't perfect, and this attitude, though essential for survival, could relax on an apparent "easy one." October 1942 brought a painful reminder that there was never a time to be lax or to assume a hazard-free operation. On this occasion we lost a recently-arrived crew on a routine reconnaissance for enemy shipping. The aircraft simply failed to return from a daylight patrol in good weather, with no radio report of distress. Our most likely assumption was an unexpected encounter with enemy aircraft or a failed attack on a U-boat. I was particularly dismayed at the loss of a flight sergeant air gunner who'd joined 233 Squadron a month or two before being lost with the crew now missing.

Flight Sergeant MacDonald was an old hand, about my own age. He'd arrived in September with a Distinguished Flying Medal; he had, by incredible good luck and skill as a gunner, completed three tours of operations with Bomber Command. This could only mean that, since the outbreak of the war, *all* of his service had been in high-risk duty where the odds of surviving the number of sorties that this man had flown were about one in twenty. My recollection is that he'd been a gunner on Whitleys, Hampton, and Wellingtons, and his document file contained nothing but glowing compliments. Along with his file came a special letter emphatically stating that he had no desire to serve anywhere except in an active squadron. A second, more curious letter from Command personnel staff contained a most unusual request: that MacDonald be judiciously screened from regular crew operations and employed in training and other non-combat duties. MacDonald himself, a quiet yet gregarious person, was unaware of this letter and its abnormal and compassionate intervention.

I was more than bemused to discover that humanity still lurked in the pragmatic heart of HQ, but my problem lay in keeping him off the operational schedule without having him assume that he was being ostracized by the crew captains and other aircrew. I told MacDonald that his special job with the squadron would be to upgrade the air gunners and to be the spare for my own crew and for a couple of other, more senior pilots. In this way he got in the air on occasion and—in a few circumstances—without my knowledge.

With his death only a month after his arrival, it was difficult to ignore a nagging feeling that somehow we had failed to adequately protect a brave man who was wholly committed to the service of his country.

CHAPTER TEN

OPERATION "LEVANTER"

October 1942: After a punishingly bland rations lunch of bully beef and canned vegetables, I walked back to the Squadron's Nissen hut office to give my digestive tract some survival exercise. Having flown a short, early-morning patrol, I was thinking of an hour or two of shopping in town but knew some reports and other drudge paperwork were overdue—including a top secret operation order concerning the preparations for Operation TORCH, which had to be studied and needed my full attention.

Yet something niggled at my ability to concentrate, an annoying restlessness of the past hour or so. Up until lunch, the day had been pretty average (that is, if any day in any war could be accepted as normal or routine)—aircraft serviceability was good, with twelve of fourteen on the line; flight operations for the afternoon were the standard anti-submarine and shipping patrols down the Mediterranean and across the western approaches. No surprises there, and no likelihood of any real trouble unless one of our crew ran into reconnaissance Ju-88s or a U-boat that decided to fight it out on the surface. None of the patrols were in close to Oran or Rabat, where vindictive Vichy French naval air arm fighters were ready to jump, at no risk to themselves, any lone Allied aircraft.

Perhaps these unsettled thoughts were a natural reaction

to the general state of growing operational intensity that pervaded the whole of the North Front Station. We had no training aids, no facilities to upgrade the aircrew, and inexperience on the job had lost us aircraft and crew. The stress of administrative chores didn't displace my turn on the flight roster; in the past month I'd flown over a hundred hours. Everybody had problems. Our station commander, himself retired from active aircrew duties, either didn't recognize the recent souring of ground-crew morale, or he didn't consider this problem worth an effort to ease work tensions.

Of course, he already had a tough job on his hands, trying to keep the small piece of real estate of RAF North Front organized so that aircraft arriving daily wouldn't congest the already crowded dispersal areas, nor interfere with the essential priority of squadron operations. And behind the heavy glasses and deadpan expression was a sincere, decent fellow in his late thirties. But his inspirational qualities and charisma were on a par with stale beer. If he kept issuing orders that confined airmen to camp to catch up on extra work details, grumbling would take on a more ominous form of disenchantment.

One particularly hated duty was the refuelling of the mobile fuel tankers, or "bowsers," which took petrol to the aircraft, a task not only physically demanding but also nauseating—and dangerous. Fuel arrived by ship in square, metal, five-gallon cans (a size and shape that enabled, among other things, buoyancy, allowing cans to float ashore to supply beach invasion sites). Whatever the reason, this didn't ease the problem experienced by overworked aircraft ground crew at North Front. We met truckloads of the cans arriving from the shipping docks and emptied them in a fenced security area, where the bowsers were positioned under a manifold trough-and-pipe contraption. Crew lifted each can individually by hand (awkward without proper handles) into receptacles that drained into the trough. There, the cans were ruptured; once empty, they were compressed in a crusher and shipped out as recycled metal.

Gas fumes abounded, and despite every precaution, the hazard of a fatal fire explosion was real. Breathing the fumes was intolerable for many and nauseating for most. The duty roster did change crews every two or three days, but the general complaint was that this was damned hard work: inefficient, wasteful, and inconsiderate. Our squadron flight sergeant had suggested to me that, with little effort, a safe and mostly labour-free system could be constructed with existing materials in less than a week. This offer was passed to the supply services 'narks' (behind-the-scenes authorities and experts) but was ignored by their sensitive egos; such can be a human attitude in war or peace. A month later, demand for fuel overwhelmed the archaic system, which was quickly replaced by some local technical ingenuity.

All in all, there had been little attempt to provide morale-boosting compensations, which can prevent a rash of new problems of the elusive kind that only disgruntled troops can ingeniously spawn. At the same time, the station commander was under pressure to keep up with his heavy and escalating administrative demands. Everyone could see the increasing numbers of aircraft and supplies arriving daily; everyone knew that something big was on the way. The uncertainty of *what*, *when*, and *who* meant a kind of nervous anticipation crept through the ranks from top to bottom. Perhaps this suspense, coupled with airmen's extra duties, lay behind the general unease.

One thing was certain: all this equipment concentrated on such a small piece of ground made us a prime target that could attract bombing raids like the one we'd had last week.

Losing crew in the air was bad; the thought of losing an entire squadron on the ground was enough to give me ill-tempered bile.

With an awareness of schedules entrenched by habit, I glanced at my watch and saw it was 1340 hours, just over two-and-a half hours since the last aircraft had got airborne. The first one should be back on the ground at about 1700 hours, and the remaining four by 1740; that would give me another couple of hours to once again read the top-secret Operation Order lying on the desk. I needed several hours to study the order, to ensure that it got firmly committed to memory and that the squadron would be ready to meet every task.

The Order itself outlined a complete plan for launching the Allied Invasion of North Africa, known as Operation TORCH. This was to be one of the major strategic offenses of the war and could well be, I thought, the turning point that would expose the underbelly of Europe to the increasing might of the combined Allied Forces. The Air Officer Commanding (AOC) had briefed me in person and in private, as security instructions for the Operation Order were clear: the only people to have its information were the actual formation commanders whose aircraft, ships, or men would be actively involved in the initial assault. The Order was to be seen by no other eyes, and the document itself was never to be left out of sight—when not being studied, it was to be placed in a double-sealed envelope and shut in the safe in the Operations Room, where there was round-the-clock security. Perhaps the extra strain on me came from this added responsibility, the enormous importance of assuring there be no security breach.

I got up from the table on one side of the room and walked across the to the window, staring at the 1,396-foot face of the Rock of Gibraltar. The top of the Rock hadn't been visible for the past hour. The wisps of cloud like smoke stream-ing off the western edge earlier in the afternoon had now become a mass of billowing cloud that obscured the top 300 feet on the western side of the Rock. No question about it, a Levanter cloud was forming.

A high masonry wall around the cemetery—Gibraltar's only burying ground—obscured any view of the lower level of the Rock; that wall and other Nissen huts blocked off the view toward the Bay of Gibraltar. But I knew visibility would remain good for some time below the cloud base. Still, this cloud had formed rapidly in the past hour. My unease burst into blinding realization: we were in for a full clamped-down Levanter that would obscure the aerodrome in fog and cloud by 1630 at the latest, with five aircraft still out

I grabbed the phone on the desk and got the weather forecaster in the headquarters operation centre at the Dockyard.

"Forecaster, this is the Officer Commanding 233 Squad-ron. What's happening to the weather? ... What do you mean, 'It's staying the same'? The Levanter build-up has doubled in the last half hour. What's the dew point spread? ... Is the easterly breeze and prevailing wind going to stay with us? ... What's the temperature lapse rate in the first thousand feet? ... Well, it sure as hell looks to me like it's going to clamp, and we're going to have a cloud on the ground within the next couple of hours.... I know it's your business to forecast the weather—can you look out the window? No, I'm not trying to tell you your job. All I know is that I've experienced the Levant situation and we've got aircraft out there. Okay. Okay. I'd appreciate a call back in the next few minutes." I hung up and walked back to the table with the Operation Order. Damn weather people, you couldn't do without 'em and you couldn't depend on 'em.

"Sir?" (Reg Goodie, one of the best Scotsman that ever came out of Edinburgh.)

"Goodie. I may have to go up to the stations' operation room for a while, but I want you to help me to remember one thing, and make sure you don't forget. You see that envelope on the table? That envelope must always be sealed before I leave this office, and it must be taken by me to the Operations Room and placed in the safe. It's never to be left out if I'm not here."

"Yes sir."

"Bring the candle and wax and we'll seal it right now." I knew I wouldn't be reading anymore this afternoon.

Flying Officer Goodie was a person with keen intelligence and perception, fully committed to the squadron's administrative routine. He was a full four years older than me, but never did he offer anything less than full support to this young Canadian squadron commander. Had his eyesight been better, he may have been accepted as air crew and not ended up as a paper basher.

When he returned to the office with sealing wax and candle, I was on the phone with the duty weather forecaster. "How can you continue to forecast unrestricted weather conditions when the bloody Levant is already several hundred feet down the Rock?"

I jammed down the switch button on top of the cradle, cutting off the call, and immediately began rattling the button to attract an operator. "Get me the senior operations controller at headquarters. Hello operations, who's the senior duty controller? Wing Commander Davis? Okay, put him on. It's OC 233 Squadron calling. Hello Bill, this is Ev Baudoux. We're running into a bit of trouble, and I want to recall the aircraft."

"What's the problem, Ev?" Bill Davis was a level-headed

type who'd just completed a tour with Catalina flying boats and could be expected to understand the problem right away.

"Bill, as you can see by the board, we've got five aircraft out, and the first one isn't due back until 1710, and the other four another half hour after that. The Levant has started to come down the Rock. She's going to clamp. We'll be in the clag by 4:30 or 5 at the latest, and if we don't recall immediately, those aircraft won't be able to get back before we're closed in solid."

"What does the weather nark say? Is he forecasting it to close down?"

"Bill, I just finished talking to him; he claims the weather is going to hold, but there's only a two-degree spread on the temperature dew-point and the prevailing wind is holding from the east, a fairly humid mass—there is no question in my mind about North Front being closed down. It's a classic pattern. You know that with this breeze just south of east, the cloud will eventually spill over into Gibraltar Bay and the whole of the North Front, for at least several hours."

"Where are you Ev, in your office?"

"Yes."

"Okay, hold on and I'll have a word with the forecaster and call you back in a couple of minutes."

While Bill Davis spoke to the forecaster, I spread sealing wax to close off the envelope with the top-secret Operations Order, so I'd be ready to leave. I could already picture the weather pattern I was certain would occur in the next two hours. With an east wind, the air mass is pushed up the sloping eastern face of Gibraltar and, in doing so, cools a few degrees, spilling over at the top, the moisture condensing into clouds. The Levanter had been a familiar sight at Gibraltar for centuries. With no spread between temperature and dew-point, the air moisture would condense and the cloud would continue to form in greater amounts and eventually reach sea level, making landing impossible.

The Hudsons were good for about eight-and-a-half hours in the air, perhaps nine if the pilots throttled back and held at a slower air speed. No matter what the conditions, those pilots had to land at Gibraltar, as the nearest friendly, available airfield lay in Cornwall, England, or in Malta, bases seven hours beyond the range of the remaining fuel, bases that may as well be on the moon.

Goodie had been standing quietly beside the open office door while the envelope was being sealed. My agitation was obvious. My usual disposition was not particularly irascible, and I took some modest pride in the official commendation that credited me with positive leadership and an exceptional operational pilot rating. I was also convinced that both air and ground crew gave me their full trust and support. Loyalty and trust in any fighting unit has to be a two-way commitment, and I believed that it was never acceptable to compromise their interests without my own interests being equally or more exposed. This concept was a basic element of the RAF officer training that came from its founding chief, Marshall of the Royal Air Force, Lord Trenchard. However, I realized that for the past couple of weeks I'd been a bit testy. Some recent crew losses may have been a cause, and comments to that effect in Goodie's journal of Squadron activities were likely valid. Several months later I read his notes of the Levanter incident, where he suggests I was more sombre and more tired than usual, that my recovery from a severe bout of the Rock's scourge was hampered by my workload.

Nothing like a few days of Gibraltar dysentery to take the excess weight off a person, and I couldn't afford to lose the seven pounds dropped in my recent affliction—and the kind that frequented the Rock was about as incapacitating as that sort of trouble can be. You spent several days with the most lightly sealed valve imaginable; it was said you could tell when a man was suffering because he didn't dare stamp his feet or sneeze when more than twenty feet away from the lavatories. Goodie claimed that he was so weak in his last attack he had to pull himself up off the thunder jug by the valve chain hanging overhead.

The phone rang again. "Baudoux here. Okay Bill, what's the word? ... What? He's still saying the weather's not going to close down? He must be daft. Bill, I know with absolute certainty it *will*.... Yes, I realize you can't take over the job of the Chief Forecaster. Okay, I'll call the AOC."

The AOC, Air Commodore Simpson, was our final authority, and it would take the aircraft between an hour and a half and an hour forty-five to get back from patrol; he'd have to make up his mind quickly if we were to recover the aircraft. I stuffed the sealed envelope in my pocket and started out through the office door and past the orderly room. "I'll be in the station ops room for the next while," I called to Goodie. "Get hold of Flying Officer Harvey, and tell him to send the squadron navigation officer to the ops room and meet me there. Office and ops room were only four hundred yards apart and we usually walked the distance, but today every minute counted; I grabbed the Hillman van and took off at the best speed the old Hillman had to give. Cleared by the security guard, I went straight to the Operations Room plotting board.

"Good afternoon, sir."

Normally polite, I didn't even stop to acknowledge the pleasantry. "Where on the patrol's sweeps are our aircraft now located? The little location pins on the plotting board were updated every half hour and were now ten minutes old on their plot position. Flight Lieutenant Blake, the squadron navigation officer, came to the door; again I didn't waste a moment. "I want the lapsed time for the aircraft from their present positions for return to base as soon as possible."

The plotting officer and the squadron navigation officer exchanged glances but without a word started to measure distance and calculate the times. On the controller's desk was a red telephone, a direct and secure line between station ops and Air Headquarters Operations Room.

I picked up the phone and was immediately greeted with a "Yes sir" from the far end; the phone orderly had to be within hands reach of that telephone at all times.

"Give me the AOC."

"Yes sir, who shall I say is calling?"

"Tell him Squadron Leader Baudoux offers his compliments and wishes to speak to him—it's urgent."

Simpson was a big ambling sort of man; he lacked the traditional crisp appearance usually associated with generals, admirals, and air marshals. His manner suited his relaxed, easygoing appearance, but there was nothing vague or ambling in Simpson's mental processes. That large, 220-pound frame with the big greying head held a shrewd person who dealt with his profession in a pragmatic and politically astute way. He was keenly aware that his present command was a testing ground for further promotion, and—barring accidents that could reflect unfavourably on his professional judgement—it was entirely likely he'd be an air vice-marshal within the year.

I knew Simpson's character; we enjoyed a good rapport. I'd happened to serve under him a year ago; at the time, he was a station commander while I was a senior night-flying instructor at a Hudson Operational Training Unit. I think that the AOC regarded me as a competent officer with some leadership abilities, although you couldn't think of this relationship of superior and subordinate as being that of friends. Still, I remembered one of his earlier escapades on a midlands RAF station where we'd both spent a fair share of our off-duty time in the Women's Auxiliary Air Force Officers quarters.

On that occasion Simpson, due to his senior rank and marital status, was trying hard to be invisible, discreet, and prudent. At the time I was suffering no such constraints and was fully enjoying the crassness of youth. I heard the story from a very lively, petite blond Flying Officer who, when not fulfilling her duties as an assistant administrator, spent considerable effort broadening my social education. Jill was a number-one morale booster, naturally cheerful, with a deep sense of ridicule about human pretences. Her serious side showed only when real tragedy came, as it too often did, in the loss of crew. When my tour of duty as a night-flying instructor ended with a posting back to squadron operations, I was struck with the fact of leaving a bright spirit, a genuine bond of friendship and mutual affection without commitment. One warmed at the thought of her, but this is to digress (another common trait of war behaviour, though then it was called 'flexibility'). According to Jill, Simpson had tripped and fallen on a clandestine visit in the queen bee's quarters, badly spraining a leg and unable to move or get back down the stairs without help. Although in pain and in a compromising situation, he could see the foolishness of his predicament and force a chuckle at the comment of the medical officer who'd been discreetly summoned to lend assistance:

"Well sir," the medical officer was reputed to have remarked, "you should be more careful when getting in and out of your car."

"The hell of it," retorted the station commander, "is that I have not been in or out of anything, so the injury is completely unearned." The medical officer's report described him, said my blond friend, as the victim of an automotive mishap; his leg was immobilized for some time.

Today the AOC enjoyed no such liberties; he was now responsible for all air activity from Lisbon covering the western approaches into the Mediterranean as far as Algiers. Arranging escorted protection of both Royal and United States Navy forces operating in the Mediterranean—and in particular the Malta convoys—was in itself a major headache for Simpson, with enemy U-boats, aircraft, and surface craft seeking target opportunities. Operational control of both the land base squadron and the flying boat squadron, together with reconnaissance units and a very heavy load of servicing and accommodating transit aircraft were also his responsibilities. Protecting the strike force assembling at Gibraltar didn't allow for anything other than the most serious and concerted attention to security and logistics for every facet under his command. The known concentration of U-boats in both the Mediterranean and the Atlantic approaches could be disastrous for our shipping and seaborne forces. With these increased commitments, he was under pressure to keep the air cover effective while making efficient use of his resources.

"What can I do for you, Baudoux?" Simpson's voice.

"Sir, as you probably know, we have five aircraft out on patrol, and from what I can see here at the North Front, it looks very much like a Levanter is coming down fast, and we'll probably be closed in by 1630 or 1700 at the latest."

"What does the forecaster say?"

"I've spoken to the forecaster and to Wing Commander

Davis. The forecaster predicts it will not come down this evening but remain much as it is."

"Well, why do you think he's wrong?"

"As you know, sir, we've been very conscious that the Levanter can be a serious hazard, and I believe that we know the conditions that precede this Levanter weather."

"What time are the aircraft due back in off patrol?"

"The first one is due down at 1700—it will have been airborne five hours and forty-five minutes—and the last aircraft is due in at 1730—it will have been airborne five hours and fifty minutes."

"Stand by the phone, Squadron Leader; I'll call you back in a few minutes."

I set the phone in its cradle and glanced at the operation-room clock: 1415. "Blake," I called, "where are the return-to-base times I'm waiting for?"

Blake looked up. "Just about ready, sir."

In a few moments he came over with a piece of paper listing the various return times of our five aircraft. The nearest one could be back at the Rock within an hour thirty of recall time; the farthest would take an hour fifty to get back. If they were recalled. With any luck, the Levanter may not clamp down until 1630, and with the AOC's permission for immediate return, they might all just make it. But we had little or no margin for indecision.

The light on the red phone flashed, and I picked up the receiver. "Yes sir?"

The AOC's voice was matter of fact. "I've just had a discussion with the Chief Forecaster, and he's confident that the cloud base will not lower any further, so in the circumstance we'll leave the aircraft on patrol and not issue any recalls."

A long silence ticked by. Five seconds, six seconds.

"Did you hear me?" he asked.

The consequences of Simpson's decision were so unacceptable I had to fight for self-control before responding. Deep down I knew, with absolute certainty, that I was facing the needless loss of five crews and aircraft. How to be more persuasive? What arguments were left?

I managed an icy "Yes sir, I understand. However, unless the bloody forecaster has no eyes in his head, he can see by looking outside that the clouds just came down the Rock another one hundred fifty to two hundred feet in the past forty minutes. I don't give a damn what he has on his charts. I know from experience that we are standing a good chance of losing five of my best crews."

I never spoke this way to a senior officer of Air Rank; I knew that I was sounding emotional rather than professional. Still I could not restrain myself. "Sir, as squadron commander it is my duty not only to operate this squadron but to assure that you know exactly what my professional opinion is without any equivocation; now I believe the responsibility is entirely yours."

"Baudoux, you are starting to sound insubordinate." The AOC's voice was brisk. "Certainly the responsibility and the decision are mine, and I made it. Now don't phone me again on this matter."

I imagine the look on my face summed up my agony, exasperation, and some hatred. The controller was about to comment on the possibility of the weather deteriorating, but the navigation officer, a discerning young man, put a restraining hand on his arm. I reached into my pocket for pipe and tobacco—and in doing so encountered an envelope: the top-secret Operation Order for TORCH that I'd forgotten to put in the Operations Room safe. This kind of forgetfulness was absolutely unacceptable; I went straight into the office and deposited the envelope in the security vault. I had to calm down and think carefully about what was to be done next.

Looking out the window over his desk, the adjutant must have seen his squadron leader coming down the road at a pace much too slow to indicate all was well; clearly, something had hit the fan.

"Tea for the C.O."

Being a junior administration officer wasn't any measure of his depth of understanding of other humans; Goodie was blessed, or perhaps burdened, with a sensitive Scottish wisdom and knew a good cup of tea was never a wrong move.

The outlook for the next few hours would be cheerless. Goodie didn't know the exact nature of the problem, just that a potential weather deterioration had been discussed in several phone calls. Nevertheless, he could see the difficulty was one of some magnitude. Our working rapport allowed him to assume the present behaviour pattern was much the same as when we'd had another fatal loss, losses that seemed unfortunately regular. When Sergeant Brent and crew had crashed into the sea two weeks ago, I again felt that somehow human values of any worth had been betrayed. Many of my friends and companions had ended their days in this seemingly endless conflict; Brent was another waste of humanity's most valuable resource: a bright, vigorous young person with high potential. He had barely reached his twentieth birthday.

After the Spanish returned the bodies that had washed up on the shoreline south of Cadiz, I went to the morgue to make official identification. Most of that night was spent writing letters to the next-of-kin trying to tell grieving families that their loss was a meaningful sacrifice to the freedom of mankind. Deep down, though, I felt nagging misgivings.

Without question the war had to be fought, but a utopian international society as a rainbow-end to bloodletting? Not likely. War is not a fertile ground for the growth of benevolence, tolerance, and compassion, except perhaps that between those bonded by service. There are some noble exceptions, but not many. And no one gets used to the crazy business of killing.

I'd be lying to say that my stress was solely due to the burden of duties. From time to time, a disturbing question, one I mostly kept pushed down, would reluctantly surface: in all honesty, could I admit that I was becoming addicted to war, and to playing with the fire of violence as the ultimate game of skill and chance? I wondered if this happened only to someone of flawed character; I wondered if the whole Nazi military fed on this addiction for power and destruction. Do all those whose blood is tainted with the warrior gene feel compelled to defy mortality in one more contest against the enemy? And this mental narcotic that rationalizes Russian roulette for its own euphoria—can it be other than the antithesis of civilization? When death brushed close, when the night was late and quiet and I was alone, these soul-searchings arose. Mostly they stayed hidden beneath my need to deal with the immediate world and to serve those who trusted me to do so.

Today, Goodie's tea couldn't quench my apprehension, the sick pangs of responsibility for the aircraft out there, the crew I couldn't order home. Impossible to think of them as statistical military units. In the brief seven months since we'd arrived at Gibraltar, a boisterous but close camaraderie coalesced around our unit's diverse characters and nationalities. Pride and loyalty had taken root, along with proficiency and individual friendships. Our growing strength and morale as a fighting unit had been tough enough to withstand the inevitable losses of the war. But the loss of *five* crews at once couldn't be contemplated without gut-wrenching concern.

In the heavy 1940 casualties in our squadron, I'd learned that emotion could be a hazard if allowed to cloud rational thinking. With survival at stake, a soft heart and a soft head are just not wartime-compatible. I tried to remember that lesson as the inevitable Levanter crept down the rock face at the North Front. I tried to focus on our present situation, thinking of logical alternatives. When the aircraft arrived back over Gibraltar sometime between 1740 and 1750 hours, they'd have two and a half to three hours of fuel, assuming reduced power while holding in the circuit. And we could expect the Levanter to persist until 2200 hours or later, dependent on lowering air temperatures to effect a clearing spread with the dew point. Obviously, the aircraft couldn't stay airborne if cloud remained after 1750 hours. It was essential to prepare the most practical contingency plans to give the aircraft crews the best chance of survival.

At 1515 hours, the swirling lower base of the cloud was down to the new gun emplacement, just slightly more than 600 feet above airfield level. There was no joy in looking out the window. Time to draft a list of the directions that would be given to ground control, flying control, intelligence, air-sea rescue, and others. The crisis would soon penetrate the operations control centre, and a furious Air Commodore Simpson would put the idling wheels in high-speed motion. Much would have to happen in very little time, and my partial preparation could be useful. In the coming flurry of activity, we had a classic circumstance for oversight and fatal error; discipline and calm must prevail.

The phone rang. Goodie answered, then called through the open door. "It's headquarters for you, sir."

I picked up the phone. "The AOC wants a word with you,

Sir," said the operations switchboard operator. Simpson came on the line.

"Baudoux, I sent out an immediate recall on your squadron aircraft. Meet me in North Front Operations Room in twenty minutes." He hung up. It was now 1530 hours.

My silent *oh shit* was somewhat bitter, his recall far too late to fix the problem that was now unfolding. In fact, it was only about fifteen minutes before the aircraft would normally be turning for home after completing their patrols.

Air Commodore Simpson's terse instruction conveyed an angry and worried senior commodore, facing the loss of experienced crews and valuable aircraft to some dim-witted staff egos. If the evening ended disastrously, he would accept full responsibility. But if we escaped the worst consequences of this foul-up, some of his operations headquarters staff would be roasted. He strode into the North Front Operations Room at 1553, behind him three sombre staff officers: the senior duty officer, the senior intelligence officer, and the ops duty navigator. I was waiting with the North Front duty ops officer, Flight Lieutenant MacBain. We didn't speak but paid the usual courtesy by coming to attention when the air commodore entered. Accompanying staff stood in the background.

"As of right now we are going to concentrate on using every resource we have to recover the patrol aircraft now returning." His first words gave the stamp of an old pro, and left no doubt this was no sickbed vigil, his voice authoritative and measured. "No reasonable possibility is to be ignored. In the next ten minutes I want a list of positive actions. They are to be screened by Squadron Leader Baudoux and approved or discarded by myself; there will be no delay in implementing the decisions.

No doubt remained about the urgency: the situation board

plotter changed the condition indicator from "serviceable" to "closed." The Levanter had descended to obscure the western two thirds of the airfield. This change in field status went unannounced, but every set of eyeballs had seen the news. Time: 1558 hours.

At 1602, I approached the controller's enclosure where Simpson had stationed himself. This small, glassed-in room, raised three feet above the ops room floor, had a long desk with three phones and a series of buttons to coordinate the constant flow of air, ground, and oceans information in the Gibraltar zone. The sliding glass fronting was not a status barrier but a noise suppressor when the controller needed to keep phone conversations clear. The glass sliders were now open; this was no time for privacy or subtlety.

The AOC was not going to make any reference to his earlier decision, and I did not expect it. When he looked directly at me, waiting for our proposed action, I was careful to keep out of my voice any tone of criticism or accusation.

"Sir, this is our proposed initial list of priority actions requiring immediate attention. If you approve, we can start work on more detailed alternatives to cover the various possibilities." I produced the draft operation order I'd mostly prepared before leaving the squadron office. The assembled operations team here had concurred with the list and sequence of priorities, made a couple of suggestions, and now waited for the AOC's go-ahead.

> ONE Message to all aircraft. Airfield weather zero zero. Save fuel ASI 130. Give fuel state overhead GIB. More info in 30 min.

> TWO Airfield security close all barriers on roads crossing runway by 1615 hours. Remain closed until further notice. Advise Independent Company Commander to

maintain communication watch with ops room North Front.

Note: Notify Governor and brief him on situation. Several thousand Spanish detained in Gibraltar past normal return home time may raise diplomatic query. Cover story needed.

THREE Air sea launch to stand by in Algeciras Bay 230 degrees one mile from west end of runway.

FOUR Call in extra communication and ops staff to strengthen ops control team. Encoding messages will have to be speedy, present duty staff will be overburdened.

FIVE Post aircrew with motor bikes to both ends of runway—visibility reports every ten minutes.

SIX Wind, temperature, and dew point readings from field level and Rock top instruments every ten minutes. Immediate report on any change that could affect Levanter condition. Duty met. officer to follow and report any trend or change in conditions.

    The AOC scanned the six action orders. "I'll phone the governor. Have the duty staff issue the orders and report the acknowledgements. We will then discuss the contingency plans and control instructions to the aircraft and any others involved."

Within twenty minutes the orders were acknowledged and the back-up staff in place. Coded messages had been transmitted to the aircraft, allotting numbers one to five in sequence of established arrival times. Their holding instructions were to circle the Rock, numbers one and two at 2,000 feet with navigation lights on, three and four at 2,500 feet, and number five at 3,000 feet, all to maintain safe horizontal separation by visual contact.

Six hundred yards away, the barricade on the road into Spain—a road that crossed the western end of the runway—was closed, stranding over three thousand Spaniards on their way home after their day's work on Gibraltar. There they stood, most carrying a long loaf of bread, the only item permitted by Spanish authorities to be taken back into Spain. They were required to be at the border between 4:30 and 5:00, and only a few with special permit allowed to remain later; an overnight stay for a Spanish citizen was a carefully monitored exception. Women made up over half of this daily migration of the shuttle work force, their clothing only marginally adequate in cool weather. The Levanter cloud on the ground and the dusk that hardened into night brought dense, wet, blowing fog and a shivering cold. Somewhere I dimly felt a passing sympathy for these people, pawns in a greater conflict. But my attention wasn't directed to the discomfort of Spanish itinerant labour; I had five aircraft and crews that would soon be circling Gibraltar with no place to land.

The Governor of Gibraltar, Lieutenant-General Sir Frank Noel Mason-Macfarlane, arrived at the Operation Room in a remarkably short time after the AOC's call. He'd clearly dropped what he was doing and lost no time en route. Although retired from active army duty, his sandy hair, craggy features, and trim six-foot frame had an air of unpretentious authority. His diplomatic manner and natural courtesy could be a deceiving image of this cool man of action. Reputable, high-level British government sources have mooted the story that, prior to the invasion of Poland, General Mason-Macfarlane had proposed to lead a covert assassination team to eliminate Adolf Hitler and thus dampen the fanatical Nazi territorial aggression. Although the story is difficult to confirm, it indicates the unseen depth of this man's character, a man many thought of as "old school."

Mason-Macfarlane was accompanied by an efficient aide-de-camp army captain, a key person who translated thought and direction into action. This captain was notorious for hearing all, knowing all, and missing nothing, his method and manner always camouflaged in pleasant convivial blandness—the perfect foil to the governor. All the clandestine activities that served British interests in the south Spain area were locked into this man's incredible memory, and on this night he could be instrumental in rescuing the crews.

The AOC briefed the governor on the problem: fuel and time limits, directions that had been given to the aircraft, airfield services, and marine rescue launches. Mason-Macfarlane was much too intelligent a man to involve himself without specific purpose; he proposed to retrieve the crews if it became necessary for them to parachute out over Spain— now the most probable course of action if the Levanter, as usual, hung around long past the aircraft fuel limit.

Our first option of parachuting the crews out over Gibraltar would almost certainly result in heavy casualties—the precipitous terrain, the wind, and the limited landing area, along with other real and deadly obstacles, made this option unacceptable. A second option was to have the aircraft ditch in the Mediterranean east of Gibraltar, also a very difficult feat in prevailing conditions of darkness and rough seas. And a third plan to parachute crews into Algeciras Bay to the west of Gibraltar was also unacceptable at night in the thick Levanter fog.

The safest place for abandoning the aircraft and parachuting in darkness into safe terrain was an area of Spain about eighteen miles north of Gibraltar. Two or three miles from any villages, it could be reached by some friendly operatives within an hour. They could signal with shielded red lights, retrieve as many aircrew as possible, and hustle them from Spain back into Gibraltar.

We discussed these options—the AOC, the governor and his aide, the senior controller, some support staff, and myself. Governor Mason-Macfarlane explained that friendly assistance at the recovery site hinged on quick action to make the necessary contacts in Spain. He gave no details, but when the AOC nodded his approval, the aide-de-camp immediately went to a security phone and put the escape escort network into action. The AOC asked me if I concurred or had anything to add. I had nothing to offer but knew, as did he, that this plan had, at best, the makings of a grim all-night vigil, with little hope of more than partial success.

A series of coded messages were sent to the aircraft, giving the final instructions: *When 30 minutes fuel remaining – Depart for position 18 mi bearing 022 M North Front – Observe three red lights in close triangle flashing letter "S" – Aircraft on auto pilot heading 140 2000 ft – bail crew quickly, wind 120/18 kts – Destroy all classified documents when leaving Gibraltar position.*

The AOC, the governor, two staff assistants, and I went to the airfield control tower to be in direct VHF radio communication with the aircraft when they came into voice transmission range. The Operations Room centre and meteorological office were on direct phone lines with the tower; we waited with the calm, disciplined behaviour of control rooms in every air command while operations are in progress. Like the calm in the eye of hurricanes, trauma experienced in the air is linked by voice and a wordless empathy to those in the control centres, who share, in turn, a close bond with their wards in the sky.

Reports at ten-minute intervals from the weather office and from observers posted at the ends of the runway didn't indicate any significant change in the Levanter condition. Conversation in the control tower was spasmodic and quiet. There was a brief discussion on security procedure and any need to relax the established tower-to-aircraft VHF voice communication rules. Every pilot knew of the presence of the Spanish observation and listening post in plain sight just eight hundred yards across the neutral ground border. We often looked at each other with binoculars, and our fellows joked that the Spanish records of North Front air movements were worth our paying them for log keeping. But our communication security system was no joke; we knew that the German espionage network of agents and informants had access to everything observed or heard (see Fig. 6).

The voice of Flying Officer Camacho broke the silence at 1645 hours. He was ten miles east of Europa Point. I'd received the AOC's permission to monitor and control all VHF transmissions. This was some comfort as it gave me personal contact with my crews. Camacho was a Canadian, a skillful Hudson pilot with a sharp mind, whom we could count on to cooperate in every possible way. He was instructed to commence right-hand circuits of the Rock at 2,000 feet, with navigation lights on. Camacho made condition reports of the extent of the Levanter and visibility east and west of the runway. The sea-state east of Gibraltar was, he said, broken with white caps. Algeciras Bay was mostly cloud-covered west of Gibraltar, the North Front airfield obscured by cloud. His transmissions were acknowledged and he was told to remain on VHF channel "C."

Over the next hour, the other four Hudsons arrived in the Gibraltar circuit at fifteen-minute intervals. Each aircraft was, in turn, instructed to maintain certain altitudes for separation. Each had remaining fuel for about two hours and forty-five minutes flying. After allowing the aircraft the smallest safety margin to arrive at the bailout location, we determined that the first aircraft would have to depart from overhead at 1910 hours and the last at 1950 hours. The ominous fact was that this unhappy process would begin in one hour and ten minutes.

As the minutes raced by, more questions surfaced: what about disposal of the cabin door? It would have to be jettisoned for crew to leave the aircraft, but nobody wanted five of these doors, complete with the emergency life raft stored in the door container, found on Spanish territory. The doors would be evidence of an infringement that could affect our undercover associates. Another question was whether the depth charges be armed to explode when the aircraft entered the water. We decided to drop the doors east of Gibraltar and to arm the depth charges to eliminate the possibility of any future incident with fishing vessels. A brief message suggested these actions but left the final decision to aircraft captains.

Weather reports were still poor but the intensity of the Levanter had stabilized. The significance of this, if there was any, wasn't given any attention. Governor Mason-Macfarlane's aide-de-camp passed him a written note. The governor told the AOC and myself that arrangements for the drop zone were in place. Somehow this information, though welcome, didn't bring much comfort.

I thought of the crew skippers, assessing their confidence and leadership in a worst-outcome scenario. Number two aircraft in the circuit was piloted by an Australian, Flying Officer Warren, his crew also Aussies, close knit and competitive; they'd support each other. On number one, Flight Sergeant Brocklebank: a worker, steady as they come. He and his crew had grown in confidence and ability, and their recent U-boat attack was a first-class effort. Barling skippered number three. He had good piloting ability and an aggressive attitude in work; a dependable crew. But Flying Officer Pat Smith, a Canadian on number four aircraft, was a different kind of character.

I think Smith enjoyed disrupting routine; still, he was perceptive and competent, very independent, non-conformist. His crew would get tough direction if need be. The seconds ticked. I recalled Smith's debriefing after his shoot-out encounter with a lone Ju-88. He'd returned from south of Majorca in an aircraft riddled with holes but with no wounded crew. The Ju-88 had been expertly flown, and Smith had misjudged his attack. A week or so before this incident, I'd discussed aggressive tactics and coordinating gun turret fire when fighting a Ju-88. Smith was unimpressed with the tactics I advocated. "Sir," he'd said, looking me straight in the eye, "would you mind running through, again, the way to successfully fight a Ju-88!"

Pat Smith's voice now crackled over the radio. "I can see the tops of the masts of ships alongside north mole and the beach at the east end of the runway."

"Standby," we shot back, "checking with observers at ends of runway."

Smith came back, "With first hundred feet of east end visible, is a downwind landing possible?"

"No possibility at this time for a downwind landing."

The chance of a downwind landing had been discussed. But unless wind speed dropped below fifteen knots and at least half the length of runway became visible, the likelihood—and consequence—of going off the side of the runway were frightening. With fuelled aircraft lined up a scant two hundred feet from the runway's sides, any collision could not only kill crew but also result in a horrendous fire and the loss of many transient aircraft crowding the dispersal parking

FIGURE II
The author talking to Lieutenat General Mason-Macfarlane
before taking him for a flight.

sites. Still, I felt uneasy about our negative reply, because if I were in that aircraft I would most certainly be considering that option.

At about 1845 hours, only twenty-five minutes of circling time was left for Greenberg to depart for bailout in Spain; four more would follow in the next forty minutes. No matter how professional our efforts, this was a gut-wrenching screwup with lives at stake. And I hated the damned complacency that had been instrumental in what was now occurring. Governor Mason-Macfarlane almost certainly didn't know the full story and probably never would—and that made no difference. But Air Commodore Simpson must be quelling some wretched thought while maintaining his air of calm. I couldn't blame him for the course of these events; it truly was not his fault.

The phone from Operations Room rang. "It's for your Squadron Leader." The tower staff controller passed the instrument to me.

"This is the duty controller, sir. We just received a priority message from the marine Rescue Launch on station in Algeciras Bay; they report that a Hudson aircraft has ditched."

I gave the necessary direction. "Get me as much detail as possible and phone back —quickly!"

The AOC had heard my side of the phone call. "What's happened?"

"One of our aircraft is down in Algeciras Bay," I answered, in a level voice that didn't sound like mine. "The Rescue Launch is there."

"Crashed?"

"The controller said 'ditched.' They'll have some details soon."

While we absorbed this jarring news, the phone rang

again. The tower controller answered and made some notes. He turned to the AOC. "Sir, the senior meteorologist reports that the Rock top anemometer indicates a wind shift backing twelve to fourteen degrees and subsiding four or five knots. He believes the change is a stable trend."

I could almost see Air Commodore Simpson make a mental leap of hope; I know I did. We were just about out of time for Greenberg. Should he be kept in the circuit? Urgent calls for observer reports from the ends of the runway brought more good news: the east end had cleared, with more than four hundred feet visibility down the runway, while at the west end, the cloud was breaking from the surface to a height of about a hundred feet. I contacted Flying Officer Camacho and asked for a visual report and for his opinion of making the runway in the existing or possibly improved conditions now forecast. He didn't hesitate to elect to remain circling over Algeciras Bay west of the runway. If the runway could not be used, he could now see the water surface in patches of light fog and could ditch safely there. This was a better worst-case option; no one had to parachute into Spain.

From that point on, the world became a place for sunrises. What had been a day of tortuous trauma now had room for bonhomie as the cloud cleared the runway in a short fifteen minutes and four aircraft landed safely. There was even more unbelievable good fortune as the Rescue Launch came in: Barling's crew had not only survived the inadvertent while-still-in-the-fog ditching, they had in fact touched the water less than five hundred feet from the launch. Pure happenstance luck. When the skipper of the boat came alongside the still-floating aircraft, he picked the crew off the wing— "They didn't even get wet!"

The next day, reporting to me, Barling explained that he could see structures emerging out of the fog and low cloud, see them well enough to line up with the runway. He thought it worth a chance to find out if there was enough visibility at sea level to pick up the west end of the runway. His crew agreed that it was no less acceptable a gamble than abandoning the aircraft and parachuting over Spain. I didn't think this could be usefully questioned, but the hazard of a conflagration crash along the runway was not a minor consideration—"Did you realize that?"

With strained humility he suggested, correctly, that nothing but water bordered the first twelve hundred feet of the west end, which was constructed out into the Bay. The aircraft was written off in unavoidable operational conditions; no questions asked.

After thanking Governor Mason-Macfarlane for his unique and deeply appreciated service, which the AOC trusted would be conveyed to our clandestine friends in Spain, we accompanied Mason-Macfarlane to his car and saluted his departure. Air Commodore Simpson then made what I considered a courteous and gracious gesture that conveyed what words could not; he extended his hand and I shook it with respect and sincerity, then saluted as he drove away. The Levanter screw-up was never again mentioned.

That night, as I hit the pillow, I sent a silent message: "God, I've never asked for your partisan intervention in this violence, but tonight I need to say thanks for what to me has been a miracle of knife-edge timing in parting the clouds. This twenty-three-year-old Squadron Commander on the Pillar of Hercules is humbly grateful."

CHAPTER ELEVEN

PREPARING
FOR TORCH

Operation TORCH was one of the most significant combined military operations of World War Two. This American and British operation, codenamed TORCH by Winston Churchill, heralded the turning point in the course of the war for western Allied forces. Its strategic purpose was to gain absolute control of the Mediterranean Sea and, by cutting off supplies to German forces in North Africa, hasten their defeat. The way would then be open to launch an attack against—to borrow another Churchill expression—"the soft underbelly of Europe."

By mid-October, preparation for a major military operation of some kind was evident in the rapid escalation of air and sea activities at Gibraltar. The importance of our anti-U-boat patrols and ship protection was emphasized by the arrival of two Hudson squadrons (48 and 500), which lent much-needed help to meet the increasing workload in patrol and escort duties. Substantial losses in the previous nine months had taken their toll in 233 Squadron. Those losses, coupled with replacement delays for tour-expired crews, placed a relentless, heavy demand on all squadron resources of aircrews and servicing personnel.

New aircrew needed about three weeks to gain on-the-job experience to familiarize themselves with North Front flying operations. This introductory overseeing was the implicit responsibility of the squadron and flight commanders and had to be reflected in mission scheduling. With newly arrived squadrons, pressure for our squadron was eased somewhat as both of the newly arrived Hudson units had experienced commanders and well-qualified crews, many on a second tour of operations. I was personally pleased to see the new arrivals for personal reasons, too, as Wing Commander Devitt (Officer Commanding of 48 Squadron) had been stationed at RAF Wick when I flew on Norwegian strikes from that base in 1940. And I'd served under Wing Commander Spotswood (Officer Commanding of 500 Squadron) at No. 6 Operational Training Unit, where he'd been my flight commander; he was not only an exceptional officer but also a friend.

The density of planes and personnel now crammed every available nook and cranny at North Front. There wasn't even a single small room for either of the new squadron OCs to use as a temporary office, so I invited them to share my office as need be. Everyone simply had to squeeze a bit more. Fortunately, because of its 12-month tenure, 233 Squadron had acquired, invented, or implemented some functional working accommodation in two Nissen huts for our aircrew and flying gear, office space, and orderly room. Once, these had seemed cramped and improvised; but in the overloaded conditions from mid-October to mid-November, we in 233 Squadron were now the *least* compressed.

Our ground crews had space in the old racing stables, where they housed tools and other handling equipment for aircraft servicing; this they did with unheralded ingenuity and the tough-love direction of Flight Sergeants Hudson and Jay, both smart, know-how guys. Aircraft storage was another matter and caused problems of its own.

In October, the large number of aircraft arriving at

Gibraltar occupied every available space, including areas uncomfortably close to the runway. More than four hundred aircraft of various sizes and types, from single-engine fighters to bombers and transports, now crowded the North Front airfield.

As part of this collection, Spitfire MKVs—enough to equip seven or eight squadrons— arrived in crates as ship's cargo. These were quickly reassembled (see Fig. 6), test-flown, then, when ready, loaded onto the aircraft carriers *Eagle* and *Wasp* for delivery to Malta (see Chapter 6). But Gibraltar's increasingly crowded airfield created new hazards, and routine flight testing in these circumstances wasn't always so... routine.

On one occasion, the flying officer pilot did a normal take-off and proceeded with the brief twenty-minute standard of settings and notes on temperature, pressure, instrument readings, and control behaviour to establish the aircraft's full serviceability. When he selected the "undercarriage down" (landing gear) for a landing clearance, a malfunction allowed only one wheel to be extended. Suddenly the routine became an emergency. Several attempts to recycle the lowering of the wheels had no success, and one was stuck firmly down.

At a normal aerodrome, with at least two runways of 6,000 feet (or longer) and larger areas of open grass bordering the runways, landing a one-wheel-down Spitfire wouldn't be too hazardous; a pilot could make a touch-down at an airspeed ten or fifteen mph greater than the usual three-point stall on landing. At this increased speed, the airplane would be flown onto the runway, or grass, with sufficient control to keep level until the wing over the retracted wheel touched the ground surface. At that contact, the propeller striking the surface would break, and the aircraft would commence an uncontrollable skid in the direction of the wing in ground contact. There could be considerable damage to the aircraft but little likelihood of the pilot being hurt. But Gibraltar was no normal aerodrome, and the situation here nowhere near as forgiving.

Parked airplanes now crowded both sides of the runway, and some would probably be damaged or destroyed by an out-of-control aircraft plowing into them. The decision to sacrifice one damaged Spitfire rather than risk losing several serviceable airplanes was the only logical choice. The pilot was instructed to bail-out over Gibraltar Bay after the crash tender boat was positioned for his recovery from the water. He'd abandon the aircraft at 2,000 feet on a southerly heading about one mile east of the harbour.

In the twenty minutes that it took to position the rescue launch, word of the Spitfire pilot's pending jump spread to many would-be spectators at North Front, myself included. There was nothing that spectacular in the abandonment of a Spitfire and the subsequent parachute descent to cause anything more than a momentary diversion from other involvements; consequently, those aware of what was happening paused and casually watched as the Spitfire flew over the runway at a slow speed with the cockpit canopy open.

When over the bay, the pilot pulled up the nose, rolled the aircraft on its back, and fell clear. The next twenty seconds had the spectators holding their breath as the pilot plunged toward the water—without any parachute opening. From our distance of about two miles, we saw no splash, but we did see the rescue launch go from full speed to a full stop in less than a half a mile.

The immediate reaction of most witnesses was "bloody hell." It was one thing to lose an aircraft in the greater interest of others but the loss of a pilot in a relatively innocuous circumstance was depressing.

Amid the frequent bad news that's part of wartime life are prized instances when some certain tragedy escapes its fatal conclusion. And on this October day, one of these bright moments had occurred. Twenty minutes after the bail-out, the duty controller in Operations Room put down the phone with a large grin and announced that our high-dive pilot had not only survived but was, apparently, unscathed. The rescue launch crew reported the pilot's first comment, after being retrieved from the water and assured of being alive:

"Damn it, chaps, I mustn't do this again!"

The remaining days of October and first week of November saw all three squadrons operating in almost impossible conditions of logistics and control overload. In addition to the overcrowding and the extra aircraft, ground crews ran continuous extra duty, and there was more and more demand for extra operational flying. (I flew about a hundred hours that month.) Yet all essential duties continued even amid this charged atmosphere that something big was about to happen: basic human needs were attended to; aircraft arrived and departed on their operational assignments; and transient crews and aircraft en route to the Middle East via west Africa were fed, serviced, and dispatched.

The most nerve-wrecking moments came when novice aircrews were arriving. Landing accidents that might damage and destroy aircraft were anticipated—and realized. In fact, for new, inexperienced transient pilots, the mishap rate was about one in twenty. Planes that overran the landing area either ended in the sea or became buried in the building rubble that extended the runway to the west. Damaged aircraft that couldn't clear the runway on their own power were literally bulldozed to one side by a crash-clearing plough truck and later cannibalized for spare parts. Human fatalities in these incidents were few but did occur.

And the arriving aircraft, with their well-known chance of landing mishap, attracted a gaggle of off-duty spectators who watched as entertainment. Human nature had not changed much from the days of gladiators in coliseums.

CHAPTER TWELVE

CRASH LANDING

The high number of landing accidents at Gibraltar was surely reason to emphasize that pilots take exceptional precautions on their approach and landing procedures. It was a point of squadron pride that throughout our entire time operating at North Front—which was never a forgiving place to land, particularly at night, in little or no wind and on a short runway with water at both ends—233 Squadron had not had a single incident of landing damage resulting from pilot error. Even without error, enemy activities or more mysterious causes took plenty of aircraft and crew.

ALL SOULS' DAY

The most heart-wrenching crash occurred on the first day of November. This most unfortunate crash into the sea was the worst of four similar occurrences amongst the many landing accidents at North Front in 1942, though the others weren't accompanied by such a high loss of life

A Liberator left Malta in the early-morning darkness, to avoid a possible encounter with enemy aircraft. A Spitfire pilot, Gordon H.T. Farquharson of Peterborough, Ontario, was one of the survivors. For him, this crash—described in a letter fifty-seven years later—is an indelible memory:

I was posted to [RAF] Abbotsinch in April '42 and was part of the group being assembled for the relief of Malta. We boarded U.S.S. Wasp in the Clyde and after an uneventful run sailed past Gibraltar and entered the Mediterranean. We took off for Malta at dawn on May 9th and landed there while an air raid was in progress.

I was shot down on October 15th and landed in the sea. After a few days in hospital I joined a group of tour-expired pilots and some women and children, and we were flown out at night in a Liberator. As you know, the aircraft crashed in the sea at Gibraltar on (or about) October 31st, 1942.

The aircraft was very full and many of the pilots, including Beurling, stood or sat in the rear portion of the fuselage.

Our baggage was placed in the bomb bay to form a bench on either side where we sat with our feet in the walk. I sat next to the rear bulk head in the bomb bay.

On the first of November I was in a Hudson, stopped along the runway with engines running, waiting for a scheduled take-off clearance on a six-hour patrol. There was no wind and either direction for take-off or landing could be used according to the control tower. The landing Liberator was half way along Gibraltar's runway and hadn't touched down; it could never stop before going over the end and into the sea.

"For God's sake, open the throttles; go around again!"

The Liberator was landing towards me, and I had a clear view of the runway. I could see that it had to commence an overshoot procedure —or crash into the water. I watched from the cockpit, a mental expletive for the pilot exploding as reflex to the pending disaster.

"He won't make it," said the navigator, sitting beside me.

At that last moment, and far too late, the pilot applied full power and tried to pull the aircraft back into the air. The Liberator stalled, momentarily airborne – then crashed into the sea about five hundred feet beyond the eastern end of the runway and the water's edge. On striking the water, its fuselage appeared, to me, to break in two parts that were visible as the splash subsided.

As the crash alarm sounded, the control tower directed me to take off immediately, to clear off the area where rescue activities would be in full operation in the search for survivors. My patrol mission, west of Lisbon, was to intercept German long-range, anti-shipping bombers and Ju-88 fighter bombers, which were attacking vessels in transit to and from the British Isles. This was not an area for other than full attention. One year later, on this same patrol mission, a very close chum who had shared a lot of tough North Sea operations with me in 1940 lost his life while defending a convoy against a multi-enemy aircraft attack. Squadron Leader Tich (A.M.) Maudsley, DFC, DFM, was on his third tour of operational duty. There were very few pilots of comparable skill and none with more courage.

In the current situation, our crews knew that other events, even the crash we'd just witnessed, must not be a distraction. Our job at hand was one that didn't allow for mental wandering or a lax attitude. Still, our patrol that day was uneventful, and the probable fate of those caught in the Liberator crash was never entirely out of mind.

At 1500 hours, after returning from our patrol and during the operations debriefing routine, I asked about the Liberator crash; it was disturbing news, involving women and children as casualties, making it more than just another 'unfortunate wartime flying accident'. In addition to the crew of six, thirty-three passengers had been en route to England. Of the four women on board, two died: one of her injuries, and the other drowned along with two babies. Three male civilians were dead, and only seventeen of the Liberator's twenty-four servicemen survived. In all, fifteen people were killed in the crash. Some of the injured who'd survived the crash had made heroic efforts to save others, described again by survivor Gordon Farquharson:

> I was aware that the aircraft had touched down at Gibraltar and commenced to go around again. Then we were in the sea. I believe I was the last person out of the aircraft and swallowed great amounts of water. I was wearing an Irvin coat, which didn't help. When I surfaced I saw two men on the port wing which was flush with the surface. I struggled to the wing and was helped by an Aussi [sic] pilot who had a badly damaged leg. Those who made it to shore were not in view and we had no idea there were other survivors. We were taken off the wing by soldiers in a rubber dinghy and transported to hospital.
>
> I had served with an Aussi pilot in 54 Squadron and for many years believed he was the person who had helped me even though I was not aware he had served in Malta. I was completely spent and suffering from delusions. It was only upon reading "Malta, the Spitfire Year" I came to realize that Eric Mahar of 185 Squadron was the man to whom I was indebted. I wrote to him in 1993 and he confirmed that this was so. My daughter met Mahar in Melbourne the following year.

A most basic safety rule, known to all pilots, is that unless there is an unmanageable emergency of aircraft control, they should abort any landing that is in the least doubtful and go off for another approach. Our squadron pilots all knew that to damage or lose an aircraft as a result of ignoring the "overshoot-and-go-around-again" rule was a degrading flying offence.

That evening, I went to the Officers' Mess for dinner and encountered two Canadians among the survivors: one was an old acquaintance, a pre-war RAF pilot who'd already lived through the Battle of France, the Battle of Britain, and the most intense air fighting in Malta; his list of victories and reputation as fighter leader was known throughout the Service. The other was Flying Officer George (Buzz) Buerling. Buerling, who'd distinguished himself over Malta as a Spitfire fighter pilot, had been wounded in air combat and his foot was now in a cast; he had swum ashore.

Needless to say, these tour-expired pilots were well acquainted with violent death as a part of their daily wartime lives, yet there was a shared anger at the cause of this crash and its pointless loss of life. Their experience as skilled, well-above-average pilots had made them aware of the sudden risk of a disastrous "prang"[†]; in fact, when the Liberator was still airborne more than halfway along the runway, some were having the same thoughts I'd had as I witnessed the pending crash: "Put on power-go-around." One survivor's tense comment went straight to the point. I would not forget it:

"What ignorant S.O.B. authorized that incompetent idiot to fly Liberators."

Among those who perished in the Liberator crash were several Spitfire pilots who had survived months of intense air fighting at Malta and were returning to England for a well-earned rest.

---

† RAF vernacular for 'crash'

GENERAL SIKORSKI

September of the following year saw another fatal Liberator accident in the very same area. In addition to the resulting fatalities, this accident also had serious political implications, as one of the dead was the highly respected and most senior Polish leader in exiled government, General Wladyslaw Sikorski. The crash occurred just after take-off. There were no survivors.

In that case, rumours of sabotage persisted for some time, despite a lack of evidence to support such speculation, which arose from the fact that some crew members were Czechs who'd escaped the German invasion of their own country and joined other exiled Czechs in the United Kingdom. Long-standing animosity between Poland and Czechoslovakia still lingered in some diehard nationalists. The cause of the crash was not obvious and remains unknown.

A BOTCHED PARADE

In another (non-fatal) landing incident, an aircraft overshot the landing strip and ended in the water, disrupting the only morning parade that I can recall at North Front in 1942. Our new station commander had thought that some visible service procedure would be useful by having a morning flag breaking and prayer parade. He wasn't a heavy disciplinarian but simply hadn't grasped that work priority at RAF North Front didn't have the personnel resources for unnecessary military drill. About forty airmen were detailed from other duties for this symbolic military ritual. I was told to serve as parade commander; the entire event would take twenty to thirty minutes.

In the small, open space two hundred to three hundred feet south of the runway, the men formed three rows facing east. Close by, several aircraft arriving from an overnight flight to the UK were landing towards the parade that I had just stood 'at ease'.

My next command: "Remove headdress—morning prayer."

The chaplain standing to my left and facing north was, at this point, supposed to step forward and face the parade. But a Wellington had just landed and was passing our location at considerable speed. The men on parade were obviously distracted, and without any formality, the chaplain—who had a similar view of the runway—suddenly exclaimed "Good God!"

Whether it was the nature and brevity of the prayer, or the general parade behaviour, I'm not sure, but I also turned to see the Wellington charging into the water. "Parade dismissed."

Fortunately, as the runway grew in length, the landing accidents diminished. Most crashes at North Front were not from obscure causes but simply resulted from inadequate piloting skills faced with landing in an airfield with punishing limits. Experience is the great teacher and in wartime is an asset acquired in conditions neither tolerant nor forgiving.

THE PILOT'S PISSERARY

Obvious pilot error aside, there were plenty of losses of aircraft and crew from enemy activities or more obscure causes. On November 1, 1942 —the same day as the Liberator crash—the Bay of Biscay saw another fatal mishap. The aircraft, piloted by a flight lieutenant en route to Gibraltar to become a flight commander with 233 Squadron, crashed into the Bay of Biscay from five thousand feet. It was daylight, and the weather was clear. Two other aircraft accompanied in loose formation; they reported that, without apparent reason or communication, the aircraft went into a steep climb, stalled, then plunged in an erratic dive into the sea; there were no survivors. The crews of all three aircraft were inexperienced replacements.

This crash was so devoid of any obvious cause that it was a subject of much speculation among squadron aircrew. The official report stated "cause unknown," but I was reasonably certain that I knew how it had happened, and I questioned most of the squadron pilots to get their opinion on my theory. With almost all fatal flying accidents, two or more conditions coincide to exacerbate the calamity. In this instance, a combination of human and aircraft behaviours seemed most probable:

1. Hudsons were sensitive to movement of weight within the length of the cabin. If a person moved from front to back, the pilot changed the trim control to prevent the nose of the aircraft from rising into a climb.
2. The toilet facility and "relief tube" were located at the rear of the cabin.
3. The elevator trim control was a small crank handle mounted to be turned in a horizontal rather than in a fore-and-aft rotation, so it wasn't user friendly for an inexperienced pilot.
4. The auto-pilot was reliable, but the control panel's small nose-up or nose-down control knob caused a very considerable change in aircraft altitude by a rotation of only a few degrees. To make suitable in-flight adjustments, some practice was needed.

5. An untrained or inexperienced pilot might disengage the auto-pilot when it had been set to maintain a level flight against the aircraft's natural trim to climb.

My theory held that the pilot left the aircraft controls to a novice non-pilot while moving to the cabin's rear relief tube, an idea supported by the observed flight behaviour of the aircraft. Once the aircraft angled into a steep climb, there'd be no chance for a person in the cabin to regain the controls. After the Bay of Biscay crash and the squadron's subsequent discussion, most 233 squadron crew decided to carry a new piece of safety equipment on all flights more than an hour long: a one-quart, large-necked, metal water bottle thereafter known as a 'pilot's pisserary'. Naturally, this created plenty of opportunity for barbed witticisms from other crew members about what some pilots were full of, most remarks not repeatable in gentle company.

In the first two years of Hudsons flying in the RAF, it was usual to have *two* pilots on a crew. One would serve as navigator but could take over the flying controls if the need arose. (In fact, many rotated their position on the crew on alternate flights.) Leaving controls to an attendant pilot wasn't a problem, but this system was obviously wasteful of pilots at a time when they were in demand, and the second pilot was replaced by a navigator without pilot training.

When new crews arrived on our squadron, they were unofficially encouraged to select the member with best natural skill to control the aircraft in an emergency if the pilot became incapacitated. It was my policy to give such gunners, wireless ops, or navigators some basic piloting experience that could improve survivability for the crew. This practice was never officially approved, but many 233 Squadron crews introduced the procedure while developing their abilities as a functioning team.

The loss of this particular transit crew in the Bay of Biscay gave me a disquieting, nagging sort of resentment about the callousness and waste of war. These feelings surfaced most often when a fatal accident resulted from inexperience or expediency rather than from direct conflict with the enemy. Why the distinction? In this particular instance, a pragmatic assessment of the crash could help other crews avoid a similarly fatal consequence of human oversight coupled with the unforgiving nature of machinery in motion. Realistically, there is never a time for pointless recriminations, which make poor mental companions in meeting daily challenges.

CHAPTER THIRTEEN

IGNITING
TORCH

In the dark night of November 8, 1942, four hours before dawn, four crews that I'd detailed for a special assignment came to the North Front Operations Room for mission briefing. We were going to drop leaflets, from about a thousand feet, over the ports of Casablanca, Port Lyautey, and Oran. The leaflets were printed in French and Arabic, with a face portrait of United States President Franklin Delano Roosevelt; the text stated that their friends the Americans were now invading the Vichy French Protectorates from Tunis to Tangier and to French-held Morocco.

At these locations, the Vichy French Navy, Army, and Air Forces had formidable military installations. The Allies' intended plan was to scatter the leaflets in close-time coordination with the actual landing of forces—leaflets and landings would happen concurrently. (At least, that was the plan.) These leaflets made no mention that British and other Allied troops would also be a major part of the force in the Algiers area. Allied leaders hoped the element of surprise, with strong diplomatic pressure on traditional French-American friendship, could avoid or at least minimize armed resistance. Any mention of British involvement would, of course, destroy this ploy; a high degree of open animosity existed between Vichy's top official and British forces, particularly in the navy.

These leaflet raids were the first of all contact operations for Operation TORCH, and their importance in implementing the policy of minimum violence in confronting Vichy forces was part of the Allied strategy for their occupation of North Africa. We took as a compliment the selection of our Squadron to deliver these warning/peace appeal leaflets, an acknowledgment of our proven professionalism. I didn't take the task lightly: all three locations for the leaflet drop were known to have substantial anti-aircraft defences from warships in the harbours and from shore-based fortifications.

The enormous formations involved in the landings were prepared and deployed with the highest security, with information rigourously guarded and given only in the case of a person's absolute need-to-know; there were no leaks. So I received my own top-secret briefing only five days before I had to have four aircraft and crews at standby for the pre-dawn task. I was not allowed to convey to crew any information that would indicate the nature or purpose of our missions.

We had no previous experience in dropping leaflets and so didn't know how difficult it would be for us to sever the loose twine that held together each of the thousand or more packets of about a hundred pages and to thrust these packets, after cutting the twine, one by one, out through the flare chute—a tube only seven inches in diameter. We had no idea how long this process would take or how damaging to our hands the dispersing of those packets would be without proper gloves. Fortunately, we all happened to carry knives that could cut twine; other than that, without any experience or procedure drill, we were left simply to do it.

I took on the most crucial raid on Casablanca, with a crew of three: Pilot Officer Esler of the Royal Australian Air Force was navigator, with Sergeants Skinner and Astor (UK) as wireless operator and gunner. These two would be our leaflet movers. Casablanca was a port city of about 700,000, with major naval facilities berthing some of France's large warships; it was known to have formidable defences.

Flying Officer Rollie Harvey's crew were set to drop leaflets in the Port Lyautey-Rabat area. An experienced Royal Canadian Air Force Officer from British Columbia, Rollie was a methodical, make-no-mistakes crew captain, whose steady, quiet manner left no doubt about performance control for himself and his crew of Flying Officer Blake and Sergeants Ash and Davies.

The third crew, Flight Sergeant Warren's, were the "force on" type who weren't intimidated by any task. A close-knit four, Warren and navigator, Flight Sergeant Summerhayes, came from Australia; their gunner and wireless sergeants from the UK. Warren's crew were responsible for the leaflet drop at Oran.

A fourth crew was delegated for follow-up reconnaissance in the Port Lyautey-Rabat area after the American landings. Flying Officer A.C. McCrady was captain, with Sergeants Bower, Currie, and Rawson a seasoned crew to give standoff cover to Allied vessels. This fourth crew was set to be airborne at 0622 hours; it was assumed that, by then, the leaflets would have been dropped and the invasion forces would be landing as McCrady and crew arrived in the patrol area.

Setting off for Casablanca in a Hudson V 9095, we passed over Morocco rather than risk an ocean approach, where invading forces were supposed to be closing in. We arrived at 0605 hours GMT and, noting a slight on-shore breeze, began to fly, at a thousand feet, a series of north-south parallel lines over the city. We had no external lights showing but needed a dim cabin light to handle the leaflets. Immediately, we saw that the task of speeding leaflets from mid-cabin to the flare chute was going to keep Skinner and Aston busy for a half hour or longer.

Flying Officer Esler kept me informed of how things were going in the cabin and helped a little with the leaflets, but I thought it more important that he stay seated beside me to direct our turning points. As the city was lit, we had no difficulty in maintaining location, but after twenty minutes the Sergeants were exhausted and Casablanca's defence anti-aircraft became aware of our presence. As the "ack-ack" came from the harbour front, I started an evasive, back-and-forth weaving to make us a more difficult target. Needless to say, our manoeuvrings were an added stress to the Sergeants, whose hands were raw with cuts and whose bodies were close to physical collapse. Luckily for us, Casablanca's searchlight coordination was ineffective; at a thousand feet, we remained an elusive target. At 0640 hours, Esler told me that the leaflets were as close to disposed of as we could manage. After thirty-five minutes over target, we set course for Gibraltar without any aircraft damage.

Our flight back was uneventful, but at the Operations Room debriefing, a distressing picture emerged. Rollie Harvey had survived the ack-ack and returned, having completed his mission, but there was no word on Warren or McCrady. As the hours crawled past all fuel endurance, we knew we had lost both crews. I knew that we were fully involved in a military operation of historic proportions, that in its successes and failures lay the future course of a war, and that all this was beyond the measure of my own difficult emotions as I tried to rationalize the loss of comrades.

Five days after the leaflet drop, I returned from a routine sweep patrol to find Warren and his crew in the squadron office. They'd been badly damaged by anti-aircraft flak and

YEAR 42 DATE	AIRCRAFT Type	No.	PILOT, OR 1ST PILOT	2ND PILOT, PUPIL OR PASSENGER	DUTY (INCLUDING RESULTS AND REMARKS)
---	---	--	---	---	---- TOTALS BROUGHT FORWARD ----
				P/o ESLER	
8	HUDSON	V-9095	SELF	Sgt. SKINNER, ASTON A/o ESLER	LEAFLET RAID - CASABLANCA
10	HUDSON	FH 448	SELF	Sgt. ASTON, MOINET P/O ESLER	A/S PATROL - MEDITERRANEAN A/S SWEEP - MEDITERRANEAN - C.L.P
11	HUDSON	FH-357	SELF	Sgt. ASTON, MOINET P/O ESLER	SUB. ATTACK + DAMAGED, ANOTHER SIGHTED A/S SWEEP - MEDITERRANEAN -
13	HUDSON	V.9129	SELF	Sgt. ASTON, MOINET P/o ESLER	A/S SWEEP - MEDITERRANEAN
14	HUDSON	V. 9129	SELF	Sgt ASTON, MOINET P/o ESLER	A/S SWEEP - ATLANTIC. C.L.P
15	HUDSON	FH-287	SELF	Sgt. ASTON, MOINET P/o ESLER	U/B ATTACK + DAMAGED, ANOTHER U/B SIGHTED
18	HUDSON	V-9169	SELF	Sgt. ASTON, MOINET P/o ESLER	A/S SWEEP - ATLANTIC
19	HUDSON	V-9129	SELF	Sgt. ASTON, MOINET P/o ESLER	A/S SWEEP - MEDITERRANEAN
23	HUDSON	FH-332	SELF	Sgt. SKINNER, ASTON P/o ESLER	AIR - TEST
23	HUDSON	FH-382	SELF	Sgt. SKINNER, ASTON P/o ESLER	GIBRALTAR - To - PORTREATH
23	HUDSON	FH-332	SELF	Sgt. SKINNER, ASTON	PORTREATH - THORNEY IS. - GOSPORT
24	HUDSON	V-9392	SELF	FOUR - CREW	GOSPORT - TO - HENDON

OPERATIONAL TIME FOR NOVEMBER = 83.35

OPERATIONAL TIME 2ND TOUR = 431.50

SUMMARY FOR NOVEMBER --- 1942

UNIT ---- 233 GR SQDRN.

DATE -- 1ST DECEMBER

SIGNATURE - .... S/L

TYPES: HUDSON

GRAND TOTAL [Cols. (1) to (10)]
1533   40
...........Hrs........... Mins.

TOTALS CARRIED FORWARD

FIGURE 12

*Page from the author's log book showing record of
leaflet drop and attack on U-boat the next day.*

forced into a crash-landing at night in the sea off Oran. Their contact with the water had been violent but survivable. The crew were able to exit the aircraft in the brief time it remained afloat, but the life raft stored in the port-side cabin door hadn't deployed, and Sergeant Robinson—who had suffered a broken arm in the crash—had to leave through the starboard over-wing exit. With his Mae West (life jacket) inflated, he managed to move through the water around the tail of the aircraft and reach the emergency life-raft release on the port side. All four men climbed into the raft; a short time later, in daylight, one of the invading destroyers took them onboard. I commended Sergeant Robertson on his crew-saving effort and asked how he managed to swim around the sinking aircraft with a broken arm.

"I don't know, Sir," he replied. "I can't swim."

VICHY AFRICAN FORCES ALERTED

At Gibraltar, the only indication of the extent and size of operation TORCH was the massive number of aircraft, which now crowded every available space on the North Front airfield.

At the same time, the magnitude of the whole conflict and the outcome of on-land battles were not part of our daily concern, as our own flight operations occupied all our energies. In November we lost six aircraft yet still completed 229 sorties. I made four U-boat attacks and flew numerous escorts on naval and merchant ships; my crew flew thirteen sorties (each six-and-a-half hours) in a three-week period, and in December this load would increase to over a hundred hours on the job. The U-boat menace had grown to demand our full effort and this, combined with the Hudson Squadrons 48 and 500 now operating from Algerian airfields, was taking a toll on numbers.

It's only in retrospect that we can see more clearly the role of our leaflet raids in the initial stage of the amphibious Allied assaults on Casablanca and Oran. In Casablanca, the landings were supposed to coincide with the leaflet drop. Just *how* this close coordination was to be managed—with radio silence of the sea essential to maintain location secrecy—has never been explained. And the planned coordination failed.

The large force of American ships lay twenty to thirty nautical miles offshore, instead of their troops and vehicles landing on the beaches during our leaflet drop. Having received the invasion announcement in these leaflets, the Casablanca-based Vichy French fleet left port to confront the Allied invasion. The resulting two days of conflict with the American fleet left the Vichy force decimated. The battleship *Jean Bart*, which was immobile but had useable 15-inch guns, was destroyed by the American battleship *Massachusetts*, and the whole French flotilla led by the cruiser *Primauguet* was sunk, with a thousand or more people lost. Captain Mercier, Skipper of the *Primauguet*, perished with his crew, following orders that he himself believed contrary to the best interests of France. The vagaries of war can be particularly cruel to a noble integrity.

We never knew who authorized the leaflet drops. The Casablanca and Oran sorties were entirely American, and in this instance, the involvement of RAF aircraft and of crew such as ourselves can only be assumed to have taken place with direct American authorization and control. The preparation and printing of the leaflets, and their delivery to

Gibraltar, seems to have had no British involvement. Some speculate that the leaflets arrived on the same American B-17 that brought Lieutenant-General Eisenhower to Gibraltar in early November. Perhaps the unhappy consequences of the leaflet drop left nobody wanting to take credit for such a thorough pre-invasion warning of the enemy. Churchill's and Eisenhower's writings record in detail the complexities of military and diplomatic problems, and both men acknowledge the air force's crucial role. But no mention is made of the leaflet raids, the botched timing, or the probable adverse effect on the loss of surprise for the Allied landing forces.

Violent combat continued at several key locations; the conflicts at Port Lyautey, Oran, Algiers, and other military installations resulted in heavy resistance and casualties on both sides. After three days, the North African Vichy military and civil authorities recognized the inevitable outcome, and resistance ceased.

Officials and military leaders within the North African French possessions and protectorates held conflicting ideas of allegiance to the Vichy government, and the Allied command's accommodation of these diverse interests was essential to consolidate control of the occupied territory. General Eisenhower had to resolve this delicate political dilemma, the task of establishing a civil and military administration and a stability that would assist (rather than impede) our military progress against the German forces in Tunisia.

Despite the ill-timed landing-leaflet coordination, Gibraltar's part in the TORCH undertaking was significant and successful. "Without the Gibraltar airfield," noted Eisenhower, "the invasion of North Africa would not have been possible."

THE TORCH FORCE

The mass of aircraft machines of various types arrived and went into action without any major organizational difficulties—no mean feat, considering the scope of this three-part operation:

A. The attacking force on the West Morocco coast sailed directly from the United States. By great good fortune, it crossed the Atlantic without being noticed by any enemy ships or U-boats. General George S. Patton commanded nine columns of warships and merchantmen carrying 35,000 troops, 250 tanks, a great number of support vehicles, and landing craft to assault beaches. Aircraft carrier Ranger and four smaller escort carriers provided cover. The troops were without experience or combat seasoning, and the navy contingent was of similar novice composition. On the cruiser Brooklyn, only nine of its sixty-five officers had more than three years in the navy, and half of the men enlisted were at sea for the first time. The fact that this force achieved its objectives deserves commendation and appreciation for judicious leadership and for the ability to cope with the screw-ups that accompany war, especially in the initial baptism of fire. Lessons from Operation TORCH were well used in the preparation of the D-day invasion of France in 1944.

B. On the night of November 6, two other military convoys passed through the Strait of Gibraltar. Both convoys had sailed from the UK and made their passage to

Message du Président des Etats Unis

Le Président des Etats Unis m'a chargé comme Général Commandant en Chef des Forces Expéditionnaires Américaines de faire parvenir aux peuples de l'Afrique française du Nord le message suivant:

Aucune nation n'est plus intimement liée, tant par l'histoire que par l'amitié profonde, au peuple de France et à ses amis que ne le sont les Etats Unis d'Amérique.

Les Américains luttent actuellement, non seulement pour assurer leur avenir, mais pour restituer les libertés et les principes démocratiques de tous ceux qui ont vécu sous le drapeau tricolore.

Nous venons chez vous pour vous libérer des conquérants qui ne désirent que vous priver à tout jamais de vos droits souverains, de votre droit à la liberté du culte, de votre droit de mener votre train de vie en paix.

Nous venons chez vous uniquement pour anéantir vos ennemis — nous ne voulons pas vous faire de mal.

Nous venons chez vous en vous assurant que nous partirons dès que la menace de l'Allemagne et de l'Italie aura été dissipée.

Je fais appel à votre sens des réalités ainsi qu'à votre idéalisme.

Ne faites rien pour entraver l'accomplissement de ce grand dessein. Aidez-nous, et l'avènement du jour de la paix universelle sera hâté.

Dwight D. Eisenhower

DWIGHT D. EISENHOWER
Lieutenant Général, Commandant en Chef
des Forces Expéditionnaires Américaines.

FIGURE 13 (BOTH PAGES)
These leaflets in French and Arabic provided by the Americans were dropped over three North African towns at the start of TORCH. Because the American fleet was delayed by bad weather, they acted more as a warning than an announcement.

رسالة من رئيس حكومة الولايات المتحدة

ان رئيس حكومة الولايات المتحدة قد طلب مني بصفتي القائد الحاكم للقوات التجريدية الامريكية ان ابلغ شعوب افريقة الفرنساوية الشمالية الرسالة الآتية :

لاترتبط اية امة مع الشعب الفرنساوى واصدقائه بروابط التاريخ والمحبة الصميمة اوثق منها بالولايات المتحدة الامريكية .

ان ما يسمى اله الامريكيون ليس سلامتهم فى المستقبل فقط بل ايضا لأن يردوا على كل من عاش تحت علم التريكلور متلهم العليا وحريتهم وديموقراطيتهم ؛

انا نجيء ، يكم لننقذكم من قاهرين مقصودهم ابادة حقوقكم الذاتية وحقوقكم المدنية وحقوقكم لحياة مطمئنة تعيشونها لاتفكر ابادة مطلقة ابدية .

نجيء ، يكم ليس لنضر بكم بل لكى نهلك اعداءكم فقط .

نجيء ، يكم ونحن نؤكد لكم اننا سننسحب فورا بعد ما ازيل عنكم ما يهددكم من المانيا وايطاليا .

الى ادعو الى احساسكم بالحقائق والى مصالحكم والى مثلكم العليا .

لا تعترضوا لهذا القصد السامي .

اعنونا يعجل يوم السلام للدنا .

Dwight D. Eisenhower

دويت د . ايزنهاور
الجنرال فى جيش الولايات المتحدة
قائد القوات التجريدية الامريكية

the Mediterranean without any significant encounter with the enemy. The first convoy held 39,000 American troops specially trained in the British Isles for Operation TORCH; they eventually captured Oran and controlled that area. The second convoy was set to land 32,000 British and Commonwealth troops and 10,000 Americans at Algiers and toward Tunis. Unknown to me, my brother Stirling, an officer with the Royal Canadian Engineers, came in this convoy. Taken together (A and B), these Atlantic and Mediterranean amphibious armadas were the most powerful sea-borne force that the world had seen, with more than 160 warships of various size and purpose.

C. Force H—the Royal Navy heavy force for the Eastern Mediterranean, designated for the protection of Operation TORCH—consisted of three cruisers (*Bermuda, Argunaulty, Sirius*); three fleet carriers (*Victoria, Formidable, Furious*); two battleships (*Duke of York, Rodney*); and the battle cruiser *Renown*.

The strange lack of German awareness of, or contact with, these enormous forces—as well as their lack of response to the obvious build-up of air strength at Gibraltar—remains a puzzle. At Gibraltar North Front, living and working conditions remained a challenge to morale for aircrew and particularly for ground crew: the food, the accommodation, the work overload, the barracks-like confinement, and the lack of destination for leave all contributed to a need for unit camaraderie and for tolerance in military protocol. We were fortunate to have a high measure of rapport between all rank levels, who shared our successes and losses along with the drab (if not outright unpleasant) food and shelter. With the onset of Operation TORCH, we now had reason to believe there'd be some relief in the chronic daily shortages and in the stress of garrison life.

In the following months, after the success of TORCH and with Allied control of all North Africa, the war went on through Tunis to Sicily, and on into Italy, where many of these troops—along with veterans of the desert—fought and defeated highly experienced German divisions in some of the most brutal battles of World War Two; these same troops later went on to form the hard core of the forces who, in 1944, crossed the English Channel to invade German-occupied Europe on D-day.

AIRLIFTING THE COMMANDER-IN-CHIEF

After a six-hour escort, I'd just finishing my debriefing when the operations officer handed me the red phone: "The AOC wants to speak with you."

"Sir, Baudoux here."

"Baudoux, can you have an aircraft ready for a VIP flight to Casablanca in an hour's time?"

I recognized this was direction, not request. "Yes Sir, our stand-by crew is available."

"Are they well experienced?"

Something special, I thought, is of concern here. "They're one of our most senior crews. I've just landed from an escort patrol, but would you prefer that I take the flight?"

"No," said the air commodore, "they'll be acceptable. But make sure they understand that every courtesy and professionalism is shown." I asked how many people would be going.

"Prepare for four, and tell the pilot he'll be having an escort of two Beaufighters."

After the call, I told Flying Officer Johnson to double-check everything for the flight and to follow all normal procedures. Shortly after, two staff cars arrived alongside the parked aircraft.

The VIP was our new Commander-in-Chief, General Dwight Eisenhower, accompanied by two others. This was the first time I'd seen the General, but in the short time since he'd arrived at Gibraltar, great things had happened under his overall command. North African occupation by Allied forces now consolidated all the actions up to Tunis, and the word from all sources was that we had the right man at the top. He knew how to get people working together, and his common sense, hard work, and courtesy put to rest the unspoken query that had lurked in many minds when he'd arrived a few days before the Operation TORCH invasion: Who is this unblooded American General? His trip to Casablanca, where the fighting had resulted in considerable casualties and damage to French naval forces, seemed part of his larger work of consolidation and mending of wounds.

A few days after the VIP airlift to Casablanca, I received a one-paragraph letter in the squadron mail, saying that the brief flight had been conducted in a professional and helpful way that was most appreciated and the crew to be commended. It was signed by General Eisenhower. I placed the letter in the squadron files and passed the General's compliment to Flying Officer Johnson and the crew. These few lines of acknowledgment for a small service were the mark of a quality leader.

COLONEL DUNCAN SANDYS

Not all leaders conducted themselves in this manner, and VIPs could prove difficult passengers at times. On the morn-

ing of December 19, 1942, I was summoned to the Operations Room for a special assignment briefing for a "courier
flight" to Algiers? I was to take "Colonel Duncan"—a pseud-
onym for Member of Parliament Duncan Sandys, Winston
Churchill's son-in-law—along with some generals from the
War Office to attend a high-level meeting in Algiers. The
flying time to the Algiers Maison Blanche aerodrome was
three hours, fifteen minutes.

The usual provisions of thermos tea, coffee, and sand-
wiches, as well as extra life jackets and parachutes, were
delivered to the aircraft. After a cursory introduction by
Air Commodore Simpson and as parachute harnesses were
fitted, I gave a summary brief of the drill in event of emergency. It was accepted with silent indifference. I couldn't
help but be aware of one general's attitude of "Driver, get this
taxi going!" The Hudson's cabin seats were not intended for
long-term comfort, and I was not moved to arrange cushions
for the comfort of this particular party of VIPs.

For about two and a half hours we flew at 5,000 feet in
relatively stable air until the sky that crossed our track ahead
was obscured by towering nimbus as far as the eye could see.
This powerful-looking squall line was going to be turbulent
but couldn't be avoided; ten or fifteen minutes of rough ride
would probably see us through to more stable air.

I told my wireless operator, Sergeant Skinner, to go to the
passengers; offer the pilot's compliments; say that we would
be encountering heavy turbulence briefly; and that the pilot
wanted to assure their safety with seat harnesses secured.
Skinner left, quickly returning with a very startled expression: one of the generals had told him that they would decide
what was necessary!

I ordered Skinner to return to the passengers and with
firm courtesy say: "The captain's responsibility for your

safety requires that he be assured of your safety before flying through the squall line turbulence." I then commenced to fly in a circle.

Skinner reported back to me that Duncan Sandys had spoken up to break the impasse.

"We can't interfere with the pilot's responsibility," Sandys had said. "We will fasten our harness."

After we landed at Maison Blanche, I didn't leave the cockpit to give courtesy to their departure. When I could see them being given VIP escort to waiting cars, I got radio control clearance and took off for the return flight to Gibraltar. The lack of courtesy by this one senior officer was the only time that I experienced a passenger attitude that lacked dignity or respect.

A post-war sequel to the Colonel Duncan flight: In 1956, I was serving with the Defence Research Board as the Assistant Chief Superintendent at the Canadian Armament Research and Development Establishment (CARDE) in Québec. A number of leading scientists and the nature of our work in military weaponry attracted visits from prominent persons from Allied countries. On one such occasion, the visitor from the United Kingdom was a Mr. Duncan Sandys.

On the day Sandys visited, the Chief Superintendent, Dr. Hugh Barrett, was absent and it fell to me to play host. The visit went well. Sandys was made aware of our world-class work on the forefront of military technology. Near the end of his visit, I was scheduled for a meeting in Québec City and accompanied him to his departure point at the Québec City airport. Earlier in the day, I'd noticed a quizzical look on his face while discussing some of our projects, so I thought it appropriate, while driving to Québec City, to mention that our second encounter was in more placid circumstance than when I'd flown him to Algiers in December 1942. He smiled and said that ever since our meeting early that morning he'd been trying to determine what caused his sense of having had some past association with me. I was surprised, as he must have met countless people in one-time encounters.

CHAPTER FOURTEEN

ST. ELMO'S FIRE

BRONCO BUSTING

At 23:00 hours on the December 18, I left RAF Portreath in Hudson FH426 for a return flight to Gibraltar. My crew of the past six months—Pilot Officer Esler, an Australian, and Sergeants Skinner and Aston—were all tour-expired; they'd stayed in England for non-operational duties, and I had with me replacements fresh from the Operational Training Unit. These wouldn't be my regular crew, but the flight gave me an opportunity to see their abilities.

The new crew pilot was Sergeant Grieves; he'd be my co-pilot on the night flight, and if conditions were good after clearing the Bay of Biscay area, he'd have a couple of hours at the controls. A second pilot wasn't usual, but on long overnight flights, the sleepless hours between two and four o'clock in the morning could be particularly tough. So having another pilot to monitor the instruments would be a relief.

Weather briefing for the route back was a mixture of cloud and turbulence passing through a moderate cold front. Any major build-up of heavy cumulus would be in the area west of Cape Finisterre, and from there we'd have mostly clear or light broken cloud. All in all, the trip would be routine, and if for any reason Gibraltar became unstable, North Africa was now Allied territory, and alternate airfields were available.

After flying three hours, we were in continuous heavy cloud at eight thousand feet when we hit the first wave of turbulence. It was only moderately bumpy, but I was relieved to have used most of the fuel from the cabin tank; although it was well secured, its weight when full was over twelve hundred pounds, so this tank wasn't our cabin cargo of choice in rough air. All other equipment and containers were lashed to the floor's strong points.

As the turbulence persisted, with more abrupt jarring and the onset of rain, it was obvious we were arriving at the cold front. I tightened my seat harness and advised the crew to do the same—and to check that all loose items were stowed. Even small, ordinary items like pencils could be dangerous if they lodged in critical locations or hit a sensitive switch.

The crew reported everything in order, but the turbulence was becoming increasingly severe. A quick scan of the panel showed that all was as it should be and the selected fuel tank was three quarters full.[†] It was time to disengage the auto-pilot and take control. The abrupt corrective action of the auto-pilot, to counter air movements, was unpleasant and put stress on the aircraft, stress that hand flying could alleviate by using less forceful control motions, a sort of roll-with-the-punch technique.

As I disengaged the auto-pilot, my eyes caught light flashing in the darkness outside. Two-thirds of the propellers were engulfed in flame, blue-orange fire shooting from the wing tips, the wing trailing-edge static dispensers trailing strings of flame.

"Close down the set," I ordered the wireless operator, "and close the trailing aerial."

In normal flight, the long cable aerial was let out from a

[†] If the tank was more empty, the negative "g's" would slosh the fuel in the tank and cause fuel starvation, so it was important to be switched on to a mostly full tank

motorized reel to give maximum range performance for the radio. But in conditions of high electrical atmosphere and lightning, the aerial became a conduit for unwanted electrical strikes. He closed it. Lightning exploded in the darkness and lit the cockpit in blinding flashes.

The turret gunner came on the intercom. "Skipper, the airplane's all on fire."

"It's static electricity," I responded. "St. Elmo's fire—no problem!"

By this time, the whole leading surfaces of the aircraft were ablaze, the windscreen a solid blue-orange with every raindrop bursting as a ball of fire. To describe the view as spectacular is like referring to heart surgery as a home remedy. ("We were bouncing around in the bowels of hell," a crew member later said.) I was busy but not too apprehensive, except for anticipating the possibility of worse to come. A fast sideways glance at my co-pilot and wireless op confirmed that they thought the devil had them. Judging from their facial expressions, their bladders were under as much stress as the aircraft.

At the first sign of St. Elmo's fire, it may have been wise to do a fast turn to a reciprocal heading to back away from the presence of an active thunderstorm, then fly at ninety degrees to the course we were on for ten minutes before resuming the original heading. This procedure gave us a good chance of avoiding the core of a storm, but it was not a sure fix. In any event, it was too late to be an option because a turn now in either direction could push us further into the heart of the storm.

In the next minute, all considerations were put on hold as we hit a massive column of violent rising air that thrust up the aircraft at fifteen hundred feet per minute. I throttled back to a low manifold pressure, but even with reduced power we kept rising at more than five hundred feet per minute. With a lot of aileron and elevator work, I was able to hold the aircraft reasonably level while riding the ascending air column. Rain and turbulence could be handled; hitting hail or heavy ice pellets was the more dangerous threat. Fortunately, the temperatures were still above freezing when we ran through the "up" air current and started the equally violent descent. With full climbing power and going down five hundred feet a minute, we "rode" the sinking air to about seven thousand feet where a more friendly sky welcomed us. Its malevolence of the past ten minutes forgiven, if not forgotten.

"Does this happen often?" asked Sergeant Grieves, after a cup of thermos tea.

I assured him that it was a rare occurrence, and that I'd had only one other encounter with a thunderstorm. Normally, we'd see warning signs, easily observed in both daylight and night flights. But where cumuli nimbus storms are forecast, flying in the vicinity is not recommended. I intended to remember that policy.

The rest of our flight to Gibraltar was routine. The new crew, though, had some interesting versions of being engulfed in St. Elmo's fire, surrounded by lightning flashes, and tossed all over the sky like leaves in the wind. They decided I was a sky-borne bronco buster!

DINNER WITH THE BOSS

Operation TORCH had consolidated control of Morocco and all of North Africa on either side of Tunisia, and after that point our anti-U-boat missions extended more towards the Atlantic shipping lanes, with a detachment of aircraft at Agadir in Southern Morocco, an experience that brought our squadron ground and air crews into contact with a very different environment and culture—and the complexity of the new and often uneasy power shift created by TORCH.

At the Agadir airfield, the French Navy air arm lay on one side of the landing area, with a base for French Army air and ground forces on the other. French Army officers and staff were most cooperative in providing the use of their very limited resources; they'd arranged accommodation for our six arriving aircraft and servicing crews, and they provided essential support facilities for fuel and secure munitions storage.

However, the French Navy commander held a different view of our presence. Although directed to support our operation, he managed to obstruct more than help. His attitude could be understood as a hold-over of French Navy animosity after the British attacks on Oran in 1940 and after years of conflict with Allied aircraft in transit to West Africa and Atlantic patrols. But in our view, our present anti-U-boat patrols in the Canary Island area were a priority that left no room for harboured antagonism.

One urgent problem for our Agadir detachment was the difficulty of retrieving cans of aviation fuel from the seashore. The containers held five gallons and were designed to float fuel ashore in areas without suitable docking facilities.[†] Here at Agadir, we were dependent on French-Moroccan troops for this task. Vehicle transport could only be provided by French Navy authorization, but they deliberately limited use of their vehicles to token appeasement, thus jeopardizing our fuel supply.

[†] This supply system was meant to support amphibious attacks, which required manpower to physically move the cans from the waterline to transport vehicles.

Two days later I returned to Gibraltar and briefed Air Commodore Simpson on the overall situation for continued operation from Agadir. My report was that the base was suitable for our detachment of five or six aircraft and, aside from the French Navy captain who commanded their base, our presence seemed welcome. Relations with that captain, however, were just short of confrontational.

Air Commodore Simpson told me to be at his residence that evening for dinner, where he'd be entertaining the French Admiral who commanded all their Moroccan air bases. Having this senior officer at Gibraltar, here to establish a working relationship, was fortuitous. Simpson told me to clearly inform the Admiral of our difficulty. I was somewhat apprehensive of how this topic would be received by this Admiral, who was the overall commander of the Moroccan air squadrons that had bombed Gibraltar and attacked our patrol aircraft.

My apprehension was unwarranted, as the Admiral's fluent English and deep-rooted hatred of the Nazis made it easy to converse without false courtesy. When made aware of the captain's attitude at Agadir, he simply said that "the man is a devoted zealot, unsuited to changing circumstances. He will be transferred to other duty." His commitment was acted on within a few days. Having dinner with the boss, where the food and wine were wartime best, seemed a superior way to resolve problems.

233 Squadron operations against U-boats in the area of the Canary Islands continued for several months, with positive results in attacks and sinkings. I made my last patrol from Agadir on February 4, 1943, feeling we'd lived through a year that saw the enemy's stranglehold on conquered territories loosened, with land victories in Egypt and Libya and with the

successful occupation of North Africa via Operation TORCH. Rommel's Africa Corps, the last of the German forces, was being driven out of Tunisia, but perhaps the most welcome turn of events to many of our sailors and airmen was the relief of Malta after the terrible sacrifices that sustained her in the brutal days of 1941–42. While U-boats continued to operate from French and Italian ports, they were now always within reach of aircraft based at airfields along the whole North African coast.

LEAVING THE ROCK

On the night of February 12, 1943, I bundled my few personal possessions into a small bag and said goodbye to some of the squadron stalwarts, who had been the unsung ground strength of the 1942 operation. I flew Hudson FH357 to England. It wasn't time for deep reflections; the war's end was not yet in sight. Still, I had a sense of achievement. 233 Squadron had met the challenge of operating from this remote strip, combated the enemy with success, and endured the loss of our comrades with pride in their sacrifice.

The past twelve months had seen the turn of the war with operation TORCH and the resulting North African victories. The new 233 Squadron commander Hugh ("Dad") Devey had been with the squadron when our first detachment arrived at Gibraltar in December 1941, and my good friend and crewmate Tich Maudsley, of 1940 operations, would be rejoining 233. The squadron would be in good hands. Flight Sergeants Hudson and Jay, gems of servicing and maintenance, would keep the serviceability standards and the morale of ground crews second to none.

My 650 hours of operational flying in the past ten months had been well spent, and for me it was time to move on.

After reporting to Coastal Command Headquarters at RAF Northolt, I was headed for Scotland to celebrate my greatest good fortune: Daphne Mary Gilmour of Montrave, Fife, was to be my bride. Our courtship, begun in 1940, had long passed any wartime romance stage. We'd become friends, and we'd found in each other the interests and values for a firm family foundation. I'd also been scrutinized by her family more rigorously than I would have been by any military tribunal.

Coastal Command Headquarters personnel staff greeted me with two positive bits of information: first, I would not return to operational flying in Coastal Command—those days were over. Second, a new Beaufighter Ferry Training Unit (304 FTU) had been established at Islay, and I was to be its commanding officer. All Beaufighters going overseas would be given special training. The need to get the FTU functional was immediate, as about thirty crews and aircraft were waiting to be processed, with more in the pipeline. I was to go there directly, but on instructions from the Air Officer Commanding Coastal Command, Air Chief Marshal Sir Philip Joubert, I was to be on leave within three weeks.

This specific direction about me coming from the very top was surprising. The Air Chief Marshal also instructed that I was to see him before leaving. He obviously knew of the casualties on 233 Squadron, which had kept me on operations for 200 hours more than the normal tour. My interview with the Chief was relaxed and informal. He asked about some of the U-boat attacks— what would be helpful to increase our detection capability and kill rates? I mentioned that on one of my attacks, I was confident that the depth charges had landed well within lethal distance of the target, and photos showed signs of structural damage to the submarine, but radio transmission that night revealed that the U-boat had survived. The analysis at Command Headquarters had assessed the drop as outside the lethal zone, but I believed the analysis to be wrong.[‡]

He asked for the chief analyst boffin (RAF slang for science expert) to come to his office. We had a ten minute discussion of the evidence that favoured my view point—but as was known, the U-boat had survived. The Air Chief Marshall thanked me for my service and wished me good fortune. With Gibraltar and Mediterranean conflicts in my past, I was off to Scotland.

[‡] Later evidence showed that the Germans had double hull modifications to some of their U-boats that gave them much better survivability to the depth charges—I had probably encountered one of the first to have the added protection.

FIGURE 14
*The author with the girl who was waiting for him, Daphne Gilmour,
who became his wife of more than 60 years.*

EPILOGUE

Over the final two and a half years of war, 233 Squadron continued to perform as a front-line fighting unit, moving from Gibraltar and Agadir to the Azores, where its anti-U-Boat attacks were significant in the North Atlantic campaign. With the successful outcome of that conflict assured, the squadron was transferred back to the UK and reequipped with Dakota aircraft to carry paratroopers and to air-drop supplies to ground forces on the D-day invasion and in the fighting in France, Belgium and Holland. 233 Squadron made outstanding and legendary efforts to supply Allied troops encircled in Arnhem, facing heavy ground fire in weather assessed as unfit for flying at the low levels essential for contact accuracy. Their commitment was recognized as an act of high professional skill and heroic determination, a continuation of their legacy of pride and sacrifice.

Shortly after taking command of 304 FTU on Islay (off the Scottish west coast), I was awarded the Distinguished Service Order (DSO) for my operational sorties and attacks while with 233 Squadron at Gibraltar. Although I hadn't given any thought to receiving special recognition for my involvements in that 1942 Mediterranean campaign, I was pleased to know that I had not failed in the challenges that took the lives of so many squadron companions who had shared the hazards for which I was honoured.

After Gibraltar and the command of 304 FTU, my only direct involvement in combat flying was with the United States Navy stationed at RAF Dunkerswell, Devon, where I served as a liaison officer to help familiarize them with anti-U-boat operations in the Bay of Biscay. I made several flights with their PB4Y (Liberator) crews, advising on surveillance and attack techniques; they were fast learners and rapidly became effective in anti-U-boat warfare. Some of the friendships I formed during that association with the United States Navy continued after the war in personal family visits.

In 1944, my aviation career took a new direction when the Royal Air Force established the world's first school for the formal training of pilots to test and prove experimental and modified aircraft. The engineering development approach to flight testing was a year of advanced flying and aerodynamic studies at the Empire Test Pilots School on the Salisbury Plains at RAF Boscombe Down. This school, the first of its type and purpose in the world, had trained eight highly qualified pilots on a six-month introductory course, and it was now assessing applicants for its first full course. They accepted three civilian pilots from aircraft industry, two from the United States Army Air Corps, two from the Royal Canadian Air Forces (RCAF), two from China, one from Poland, one from Norway, two New Zealanders, one Australian, one South African and nine from the Royal Air Force. All had to have exceptional or above average piloting ability and experience. I was fortunate to be one of the RAF applicants accepted; the course was considered to be the pinnacle of world aviation training.

Still, even here the work was dangerous and there were unfortunate casualties. One British, an Australian and one RCAF Canadian were killed during the course, while the other RCAF Canadian had a disqualification incident. These unhappy occurrences left me as the only Canadian, (though still an RAF officer) to have completed the qualification. I'd also begun flying the first Allied jet fighter: the Gloster

Meteor. With two RCAF candidates having met disaster and misfortune, an arrangement was made for my transfer to the RCAF. This evolved into post-war service back home in Canada as the first formally trained Canadian Test Pilot, and I piloted the first jet fighter in Canada at St. Hubert, Québec, in September 1945.

ACKNOWLEDGEMENTS

From conception to final publishing this book took longer than originally planned. The mental dredging and process of retrieving history is always subject to interpretations of some events that vary according to the viewpoint of the participant or witness. The time needed to determine consensus and validity, added to personal priorities, at times suspended manuscript writing. However, the support and encouragement of air force veterans, who shared their experiences of war-time 1942 at Gibraltar, added depth to the stories and feeling to the human struggle in that year-long episode of World War Two. Renewed contacts with some old comrades were not only helpful in refreshing memories but provided vivid first-hand accounts of enemy encounters, war's tragedies, human idiosyncrasies, phobias, resilience, sacrifice, compassion, and the commitment of those youthful spirits.

The list of contributors to the book material is too lengthy to do full justice to all, but some must be mentioned. In addition to the verification of research in the Kew Archives of London, England, a number of old colleagues were specific where records were sketchy or ambiguous. The 233 Squadron Association, through its secretary, Ken Harper, was a major source of documents that gave post-war versions of attacks and losses as they became available from German, Spanish and other sources.

Here in Canada, a number of the contributors must be given special thanks. Jim Kennedy of Victoria, British Columbia; Bob Shimmell of Lancaster, Ontario; Gordon Farquharson of Peterborough, Ontario; and Robert J.A.

Smith of Vancouver, British Columbia were among the many whose stories captured our lives at Gibraltar when that place was a remote keystone to the course of the war.

I must express gratitude to those who kept the machinery of the writing process in motion; typing, assembly and editing thousands of words that formed the manuscript was only possible with the stalwart help of colleagues. Gina Markie, who from start to final draft typed, organized and stored all that the book contains. The editing of the manuscript was left to Clare Goulet. Her attention to structures and flow were essential to the final form and presentation of the story.

The work of compiling and arranging illustrations and final formats with the printer were left to the perseverance of my daughter, Jane MacKay, who fully earned her father's thanks.

If the book is considered informative, readable and entertaining I am in their debt.